FAITH FITNESS

Ignite the Power of a Fit Church Culture

Cecil Sharp

Dedication

To Patti, my wife, life, and sentry, and to our children's children,
the next generation

Preface

Faith Fitness was inspired during my daily devotionals while reading *A Guide to Prayer for Ministers and Other Servants* by Rueben P. Job and Norman Shawchuck. Out of my growing concern for our churches, I began a journey of seeking to understand the church's missional role in the United States. I uncovered too many churches that were struggling to exist, much less do the will of the Father. I looked closer at the roles both of ordained leadership and non-ordained leadership in churches by studying the subject from the quadrilateral of Scripture, tradition, experience, and reason. My investigation suggested that over time many churches lose their level of spiritual fitness and intimacy with the Lord and develop a dysfunctional heart. I also discovered some healthy churches that lacked the ability to reproduce fit followers.

Constant prayer, persistent study, and the spiritual wisdom of many saints provided insight into the ingredients of ecclesial fitness. My background in medicine and organizational structure helped me create a fresh look at church culture. Providing a biblically based model that leadership can understand, teach, and use as a tool to develop fit followers will help reestablish the heart of Christ and ignite the power of the Holy Spirit in churches once again. I hope that the concepts I present in *Faith Fitness* will help dysfunctional churches restore their fortunes and inspire healthy churches to attain the highest level of fitness.

Besides everything else, I face daily the pressure
of my concern for all the churches.
Paul[1]

Contents

Charts and Diagrams

Introduction

Restore our fortunes, Lord,
like streams in the Negev.
Psalm 126:4

Five generations of Americans are now living together concurrently, and each generation strives for its own version of a relevant and intimate relationship with Jesus Christ. The culture among leadership in some churches has limited its effectiveness in drawing unbelievers and connecting to community. The result is dropping worship attendance and congregational participation. The dwindling pools of revenue are straining church budgets, denominational retirement accounts, ministry programing, and mission opportunities. Exacting more commitment out of declining memberships has not been the answer. Jesus said that no one pours new wine into old wineskins. If they do, the wine and the wineskins will be ruined.[1] So why do church leaders continue to pour ideas into their old church mind-sets, behaviors, and practices?

Faith Fitness is a resource that unlocks the mystery of church organizational health by teaching church leaders the strategies that will improve their church's culture in order to welcome the Holy Spirit, build member enthusiasm, and focus on the unique purpose of their churches. *Faith Fitness* gives church leaders tools to create the type of organizational culture that will draw new members and train them to become fit followers.

It was written for ordained and non-ordained church leaders by a member of the laity. Let me tell you why I am an ideal candidate to write a book on church health and fitness. I am a physician who has cared for the health of critically ill newborns for the past thirty-three years. I've served on every church committee as well as strategic planning committees. I haven't been called into ordained ministry, but I've been called to care about the health of newborns and organizations. A physician's executive MBA helped me win accolades for helping medical practices. I've used a second MBA with an emphasis in organizational behavior to elevate organizational performance in churches.[2]

In addition to visiting churches and speaking with clergy from nearly every faith tribe, I partnered with an economics professor for a three-year period to study church enthusiasm and congregational growth of over eight hundred churches. The results were published in a leading economics journal.[3] I helped birth and have been a resource for one on the fastest growing churches in Georgia. Now I want to share my knowledge. My vision is for every church to have a fit culture, and my mission is to help churches reach their next level of fitness. My focus is to develop leaders into worthy followers and give them a pathway to improve the health and purpose of their churches.

The first chapter, "The Journey," discusses the preparation and difficulty of taking the fitness journey. It also introduces the prescription found at the end of each chapter. The series of prescriptions provides a healing template for sojourners to increase their faith, transform into worthy leaders, and then lead their own *ekklesia* (a Greek word meaning "congregation") to a fitness lifestyle.

The chapter on "Church Culture" not only describes the unhealthy culture within so many churches today but also provides the ingredients of a healthy church culture as found in three New Testament churches. A fit church archetype is created from these churches. The spectrum of organizational fitness among churches is also discussed: nominal, languid, wellness-oriented, and fit. The spectrum was derived from the Revelation churches and from my experience and research. Readers will learn the differences between each church culture and how they can help their church climb from one level to the next.

"Understanding Fitness" provides leaders with the definitions of and distinctions between the terms "health," "wellness," "fit," optimal fitness," and "enthusiasm." This chapter gives useful information about fluctuating worship attendance, the importance of enthusiasm among members, and the concepts of church extinction, recovery, and rival growth. Finally, disease and its detrimental effect on church fitness is discussed.

The chapter on "Fitness Toolbox" is a unique leader resource that can be used for strategic planning, increasing worship attendance and congregational growth, and connecting to the community. Combining insight from biblical metaphors on the church, from the tradition and experience of thirty ordained theologians and from the reason of academic researchers, a hierarchy of important drivers that contribute to church health and growth become leadership tools.

The final two chapters, "Fit Body" and "Fitness Lifestyle," use a fitness model to help churches operate with a fit culture. Leaders will learn the communication style, fitness habits, and training methods used in wellness-oriented churches that aspire to become follower training sites. By adopting the training methods described, churches transform into vibrant centers with enthusiastic believers.

Every chapter, along with its accompanying prescription, has a series of questions that can be found in an appendix called "Fitness Exercises." The exercises allow readers to experience the fitness journey with other leaders from their church. Group study can accelerate personal development and create teamwork among sojourners. Study questions about each *Faith Fitness* principle serve as a type of spiritual workout or community "work-in" session that I call *Ruach*, which is Hebrew for "breath" or "Spirit," because it invites the Holy Spirit to guide the workout while participants discuss the material. The fitness exercises give leaders an opportunity to learn about the fitness tools and initiate strategies for improving organizational health.

Are you a member of the ordained clergy or a member of the laity who is frustrated with your church's declining membership, aging congregation, or lack of enthusiasm? Do you want a healthy church culture so that members can enthusiastically share the love of Jesus Christ? You finally have a resource, *Faith Fitness,* that can give you step-by-step instructions on how to build a healthy organization and use it to draw new, younger members. This book will give leadership the tools to ascend the fitness spectrum, regardless of their starting level of fitness. Some churches are growing, but their leaders have difficulty in ascending to the highest level of fitness. By following the directions in *Faith Fitness*, you can transform your ekklesia into a fit church, so the ecclesial DNA of the gospel can be multiplied by building up or planting new churches.

Statistically, every thirty-five minutes of the day a church in the United States closes its doors.[4] Other churches teeter on the precipice of irreversible decline. Do not wait to claim the healing and health that your church deserves. God has a history of using ordinary people to be extraordinary conduits of his love. Keep an open mind and heart. You may be given the spiritual authority and empowerment to lead your church to a wellness orientation and a fitness lifestyle.

"For I know the plans I have for you," declares the Lord,
"plans to prosper you and not to harm you,
plans to give you hope and a future."
Jeremiah 29:11

Head, Heart, Hands
Rx   Breath of Holy Spirit
Tradition // scripture — ◇ = Reason — avoid anti intel!
experience
4D BOOKS
Post Modern Era

THE JOURNEY

God is greater than our hearts,
and he knows everything.
1 John 3:20

Post Modern
Modernity
1860 →

Post Modern 1980's

Explosion of Communication 1987 ("1960's") 1986 - 2019 - Post Modern Era

On May 12, 2005, Ed Viesturs completed an eighteen-year project when he summited Annapurna, one of only fourteen mountain peaks higher than 8,000 meters (15,000 feet). Mountain climbers are distinguished as "elite" among their peers if they have summited all fourteen of these peaks. Only four climbers have accomplished this amazing feat without oxygen. Ed Viesturs is one of them.

Annapurna is a Sanskrit name derived from an ancient goddess known as the "provider." It is one of the most treacherous of the Himalayan massifs (a compact group of mountains). Known for sudden and unexpected avalanches, the peak has the highest mortality rate among climbers in the world. While Everest is the highest and most well-known peak, and its neighbor K2 is touted as the most technical, Annapurna is the most dangerous. A new reality program about helicopter pilots rescuing climbers from Everest underscores the danger of climbing above 8,000 meters, an altitude known as the death zone.[1]

Viesturs was inspired to become a mountain climber as a little boy after reading a book entitled *Annapurna* by Maurice Herzog, the first climber to summit an 8K meter peak (1950). Viesturs managed to climb all the other thirteen peaks over his career. Annapurna, the first major peak ever climbed, was now the last and most menacing for Viesturs. This mountain would define his career. Herzog describes the overwhelming odds against summiting Annapurna, and, comparing the mountain with life's challenges, he ends his book by observing, "We all have our own Annapurnas." After two failed attempts and a lifetime of climbing experience on the world's highest peaks, Viesturs "wanted to go back to Annapurna and let the mountain tell me what to do."[2]

Typically, climbers set up multiple camps over multiple weeks to increase their chances of making a summit. In what became an unconventional maneuver, Ed Viesturs and his team sprinted to the summit of Annapurna in a three-day climb, carrying equipment along the way. Viesturs said the most important lesson he learned from summiting the world's tallest peaks was "listen to the mountain." By listening to Annapurna, Viesturs learned how to safely summit and get back down from "the largest test of my life."

Viesturs' goal was to climb the world's tallest peaks. As Christians, what is our goal? What is our purpose? Some would simply say to know God. The Church offers the ultimate mountain experience where the true provider, Jesus Christ, is found. Awaiting the adventurer is a deeper knowledge of God. The trek leads to a place where God speaks to his children. Much like Abraham on Mount Moriah, Elijah on Mount Horeb, or Moses on Mount Sinai, the summit is a place where God's voice is heard away from the noise of the world. It was on another peak, Calvary, where God created the permanent meeting place between God and man. The church "mountain" also gives believers a chance to renew their fellowship with God.

Starting any climb can be hard. The base of most mountains is difficult to traverse because it accumulates glacial debris. This moraine changes constantly, just like the social changes within our society. Social media, virtual life, and loose but connected horizontal relationships have become the norm. Churches have difficulty navigating this territory without a reliable map, and many have lost their way. *Faith Fitness* introduces a pathway through the moraine so making the summit is possible.

Our journey will have its challenges. We'll be part of a team of leaders attempting to ascend the mountain of change necessary to achieve the understanding of church fitness. To successfully summit, we must develop a fit heart by practicing spiritual fitness, acclimatize to the altitude of change by training in holiness, and harness to the mountain by listening to the real provider, the Lord Jesus Christ. He will endow us with a hope to meet our challenges that is not based upon unfounded optimism, but on the blessed assurance of our destiny. The motivation and ability to accomplish the task comes from the power of the Holy Spirit.

A fitness lifestyle is a biblical goal, and the pathway only becomes possible through God. The path is passable because, "Every valley shall be raised up, every mountain and hill made low; the rough ground shall become level, the rugged places a plain."[3] Exercise your faith now and the supernatural power of the Holy Spirit will restore your fortunes. Turn the kaleidoscope of commitment and enjoy the colors of obedience radiating from within your church. God wants to regenerate the heart of your ekklesia[4] into the heart of Christ, but to take the journey you must listen to the provider.

Journey Preparation

One of my passions is paddling. Solitude on a body of water with my paddle rhythmically and quietly slicing me toward the sky's reflection on the water is rejuvenating. On occasion, I guide a trip on the South Carolina coast where a small group camps upon one of the thousands of small islands or spits far from city lights, life's bustle, and personal troubles. Packing for such a trip is challenging, for a kayak allows limited space for supplies. The general rule is to carry only essentials. The conveniences of home are left behind, because packing is all about the trip.

As you read this book, you too will be taking a journey: one that I call *Faith Fitness*. The adventure is over new territory, a new moraine created by the postmodern era. The trip is designed as a group outing, but you will have a very personal experience. Preparing for this trip requires three elements: packing equipment, charting the course, and following instructions.

Equipment Checklist

The equipment list is short. We are only taking the Word of God and this *Faith Fitness* book. God's Word will provide the required nourishment for the trip. As 2 Timothy 3:16-17 tells us, "All Scripture is God-breathed and is useful for teaching, rebuking, correcting and training in righteousness, so that the servant of God may be thoroughly equipped for every good work." Proverbs 2:6 similarly reminds us, "For the Lord gives wisdom; from his mouth come knowledge and understanding."

The fitness exercises in Appendix 4 allow small groups to study and discuss the organizational principles found in *Faith Fitness*. Groups can self-pace through the exercises, and leaders can be accountable to each other as they move through them. Small groups collectively answer questions and debrief on the organizational and spiritual principles. By participating in the exercises, leaders will use the skills to build strategies that will improve fitness in their churches.

Our backpacks must not be overweight, or they will slow or stop our progress. Only essentials should be taken. Therefore, we are challenged to leave all our church baggage and biases at home. This is a new adventure with new experiences.

Charting the Course

One of the most exciting parts of paddling is choosing where to paddle. The trip length, season, weather, wind, tide, current, and the expertise of the other paddlers must be taken into consideration. Charting the course and planning for a safe trip so that all the participants get the most benefit and enjoyment is an art form. Our faith fitness journey is no different. It is designed for Christians like you who serve in some capacity in your church. The journey is for ordained clergy as well as laity. During the trip, we will discover the difference between healthy and unhealthy churches, the drivers for church wellness, and the transformative power of the fitness lifestyle.

The Israelites had a long and remarkable journey during their Exodus experience. While near Mount Horeb, the Lord would speak to Moses at his campsite outside a special tent that was called the "tent of meeting." It was at this meeting that Moses learned of God's will for his people.[5]

For touring kayakers, the reward for a long day's paddle is sitting outside their tents by a crackling fire while debriefing on the day's activities and sights. We too will pause and rest along the way.

Follow Instructions

Paddling looks easy and fun to the recreational paddler on a warm day with still waters and beautiful weather. Most journeys, however, have varying levels of difficulty. To overcome the challenge of guiding many participants with different skill levels, I've learned that the most important (and required) trait in a sojourner is **teachability**. During times of adversity, safety and health are the priority. The participant must stay close to, pay attention to, and listen carefully to the guide. These instructions are very important, so let's spend time on the ingredients of a teachable team member.

Derek Prince, a British medical orderly who developed a serious illness while stationed in the deserts of North Africa during World War II, found a personal relationship with Jesus Christ, along with a key to healing, by listening carefully to a special passage of Scripture. He called the healing qualities he found in the words of Proverbs 4:20-23 "*God's Medicine Bottle,*" and he wrote a book by that name.[6] Let's see how the principles in God's medicine bottle can build the qualities of teachability.

My son, pay attention to what I say; turn your ear to my words.
Do not let them out of your sight, keep them within your heart; for they are
life to those who find them and health to one's whole body. Above all else,
guard your heart, for everything you do flows from it.
Solomon[7]

Pay attention. When Moses led the Israelites out of Egypt, God told Moses to pay attention, listen carefully to his voice, and follow all of his directions. Moses did a great job, but he wasn't allowed into the Promised Land at the very end of his life because he added one step to God's instructions and took matters into his own hands.[8] Two of Aaron's sons, Nadab and Abihu, added incense to their censers and offered unauthorized fire before the Lord. Again, for adding to the Word, God sent fire to consume them and they died.[9] Faith comes from paying attention.

Paying attention means that we are focused on Christ and nothing else. When I was growing up, television was very novel. I looked forward to the comic television show *Get Smart*. When clumsy secret agent Max needed the attention of his boss, a large clear plastic bubble, the cone of silence, descended from the ceiling to cover them in privacy. It suited the corny humor of the show. Sometimes we need a symbolic "cone of silence" to force out the noise of the world so we can focus privately on the words of Christ. Find your cone of silence and use it! Others have no right to interrupt or deny the claim of renewal that God has in store for you. God's Word works in us only insofar as we receive it.

We must learn how to be active listeners, not passive. On my first day of fifth grade, after lunch during English class, my teacher invited the class to participate in an exercise that I remember to this day. She asked us to get out a sheet of paper and pencil, sit quietly, and write down every sound we heard. I was not used to the quiet. It was almost painful. Our compliant class obediently carried out the task for ten long grueling minutes. I wrote down six sounds during that time. Everyone shared their results, which were mostly local sounds within our classroom.

Our teacher then instructed us that listening was an active process; it took energy. "We must listen intently in order to hear," she would say. She invited us to repeat the exercise. The next ten minutes flew by. Despite writing feverishly, I could not keep up with the many sounds that filled my ears; I had amassed twenty-four sounds during the assignment. The class was abuzz when we debriefed the second time. Now we could hear sounds outside the classroom, as far as across the street from the school.

The disciples followed Jesus and listened to him daily, yet after the resurrection they seemed lost. They returned to their boat and to the only other thing they knew: fishing. Then John recognized Jesus calling from the shore, saying, "Throw your net on the right side of the boat and you will find some." Peter had not recognized the Lord.[10] Paying attention takes solitude, focus, and intention.

Bring the right attitude. Derek Prince said, "By laying down our preconceptions and prejudices, bending our stiff necks and opening our ears, we become able to listen carefully to what God says and not reject it because it doesn't agree with something we thought God ought to have said."[11] Come with the right attitude. Come expecting to learn the most important thing that you'll ever learn. The attitude you bring is important to learning.

Waynesboro, Georgia, which is one of the towns near where I live now, claims to be the bird dog capital of the world. Good bird dogs have the attitude of natural and gifted hunters. They position their head and ears to maximize scent and sound. They live to discover the prize that awaits their effort. When it is found, the bird dog freezes and focuses upon it until the prize is taken. Likewise, we must incline our head and bend our ears in an attitude of humility and teachability so that we can maximize our learning experience.

A teachable attitude puts us in close proximity to the one doing the teaching. To receive instructions correctly, we must be receptive to the information and be willing to participate fully. You're taking an important journey. Like Viesturs when he ascended Annapurna, it's time to leave camp and begin. The difficulty is high, but the rewards are great. Do not lose heart. For the Lord goes out before you to lead you like he led his children in the wilderness.[12] You and other leaders of your church are ready. You can do this.

Prescriptions

An important part of this book is the spiritual exercises that are expressed as a prescription, Rx, at the end of each chapter. The exercises are treated as a prescription because the word means advice authoritatively recommended for the purpose of bringing healing or health to the recipient. It is specifically addressed to the spiritual heart of the leader or the leader's ekklesia. Just like my personal doctor's prescriptions are meant to bring me health, the Rx in *Faith Fitness* will make you healthier too. Each prescriptive exercise stands alone and works sequentially with the others. The exercises must be accomplished in order and followed carefully. Don't bury this treasure in a field, promising you'll come back one day.[13] Adhere to the advice on the exercise prescription itself, "No Substitution Permitted." Please take as directed.

There are no shortcuts in life. At one time or another we've all put considerable energy into looking for a shortcut that simply doesn't exist. Most patients want to take a shortcut too. They say, "If I could just order my own tests and call in my own prescription, I wouldn't need the doctor." A shortcut would be nice.

I enjoy working with my hands. I've been renovating a small house located at a nearby lake that my wife and I affectionately call "Sanctuary", because it is such a blessed and restful place for us. As we tackle each new room, we collect ideas from TV shows like *Design on a Dime*, *Fixer Upper*, or *Ask This Old House*. The hosts always carry out the makeovers in an effortless and fluid manner within the time frame of the show. In real life, this is not so.

Any church trying to become healthier, change culture, and ascend the fitness spectrum may experience a process of demolition and reconstruction, which may be painstakingly slow and sometimes painful. Restoring the spiritual life of a church sometimes requires an operation on the heart. Henri Nouwen says: "Indeed, living a spiritual life requires a change of heart a conversion. Such a conversion may be marked by a sudden inner change or it can take place through a long, quiet process of transformation."[14] Though Nouwen is talking about the heart of the individual believer, his truth is applicable to the whole church body.

Some churches do not need complete reconstruction or heart transplantation. These churches just need a little "tender loving care" to reconnect with the heart of Jesus. Sometimes a small adjustment will provide a large result. Churches need to make the adjustment. The prescription(s) will also help healthy churches that may only need some preventive maintenance.

> Whoever belongs to God hears what God says. The
> reason you do not hear is that you do not belong to God.
> Jesus[15]

Fitness Moment

- We are now living in the postmodern era, and our churches must learn to navigate this new moraine.
- Organizational improvement is primarily up to church leaders.
- Every church has challenges. Leadership must unify and submit to the Lord if they are to help their church summit over these changes.
- By creating a teachable attitude and truly listening to the Lord, the provider, our churches can journey toward faith fitness and doing his will.
- Our first prescription is to rest in the Lord.

Rest

Sig: *follow the instructions*
Refill(s): *prn – as needed*
Comments: *No substitutions permitted*

Thou hast made us for thyself, O Lord;
and our heart is restless until it finds its rest in thee.
St. Augustine

Our journey in *Faith Fitness* is just starting. This prescription is designed for the reader to pause, contemplate, pray, and discern the will of God so that personal growth and church health can be achieved. Rest is the first step in self-preservation, healing, and growth. The purpose in reading *Faith Fitness* is to acquire organizational and leadership skills so that the will of God may be enacted in your church, so your church can become healthier. We're not taking this journey alone, and we don't have to be alone during every rest period. Resting in the presence of the Lord is important. It is the ideal time for prayer, reading the Word, and participating in the Ruach exercises included in Appendix 4.

Bob Buford has written a book called *Halftime*.[16] In it he says we should get off the playing field of life and go into the locker room. During halftime we can rest, evaluate the first half, and make adjustments for the second half. In this case, the second half may be after any significant life change. A church body is no different than the human body. The habit of retreat and rest creates a space and a time when God can speak to us.

It was during rest when Christ moved away from the crowd to a hillside so he could pray and talk to the Father.[17] Jesus invites us to, "Come with me by yourselves to a quiet place and get some rest."[18] Jeremiah encouraged his people to, "Stand at the crossroads and look; ask for the ancient paths, ask where the good way is, and walk in it, and you will find rest for your souls."[19] It is beside the campfire that our gear is accessed, repaired, and prepared for the next day. In the same way, each sojourner should heal their sores and blisters and rest along the way.

As a physician, I know that the human body heals best when it is resting. I am very impressed with the healing properties of the human body. Consider the process of healing after a simple injury. First, an injurious agent like trauma, heat, or infection creates a wound that results in tissue damage. Host defense mechanisms pour into the wound, creating the swelling that is characteristic of an inflammatory response. Rest prevents further tissue damage, and allows the healing to start. Regenerative tissue completes the healing. Similarly, we must stop and listen to the Lord, who will start to heal us. Our busy lifestyle demands that we occasionally stop, rest, and repair.

During the Exodus, the Lord allowed the nation of Israel to stop and rest frequently after they left Egypt. It was their time to refuel, debrief, and heal. The Lord resided in a fire outside a tent set aside from the others. The "tent of meeting" was the place for leaders to receive instruction from the Lord.[20] The heart of a church may eventually fail, but during rest an infirm church may be strengthened by the Lord.[21] The first step in spiritual fitness is to rest in the Lord.

You're taking an important journey. If you're reading this material alone, then enlist (or perhaps lead) others to take this fitness journey with you. By understanding the principles in *Faith Fitness,* by following the prescriptive advice at the end of each chapter, and by participating in the fitness exercises (Appendix 4) with other church leaders, you'll have the tools to ascend the mountain of change ahead.

If the body is able to rest, then the water that Jesus gives us "will become in him a spring of living water welling up to eternal life"[22] and "streams of living water will flow from within him."[23] As you take this fitness journey, rest in the Lord. My prayer for you is that, "Whether you turn to the right or to the left, your ears will hear a voice behind you saying, 'This is the way; walk in it.'"[24]

2

CHURCH CULTURE

Test me, Lord, and try me, examine my heart and my mind;
for I have always been mindful of your unfailing love and have lived in reliance
on your faithfulness.
Psalm 26:2–3

Organizational culture is defined as the set of shared attitudes, values, goals, and practices that characterize an organization.[1] Culture is important because the beliefs and behaviors of people guide their actions. A technology business like Google prizes creativity and innovation. Pictures inside Google's work space, Googleplex, look more like an adult playground, with video games, nap pods, a gym, swimming pools, and ping-pong tables. Every meal is free and organic! Google's culture is flexible, fun, and focused on employee happiness. Instead of a Human Resources Department, they have a People Operation's Center.[2] Culture is a system that has input and output. Google has a culture that results in creativity and innovation.

Fitness centers have their own brands and cultures for their customers. Gold's Gym™ has a traditional model, with free weights for individuals to build strength.

The Pure Barre™ brand offers isometric movements using ballet barres, and it stresses technique, community, and empowerment to build bodies and change lives. The CrossFit™ brand offers a fun and competitive community, online nutritional information with support, and workout sessions using a "WOD" or workout of the day. The culture of each brand attracts a different clientele and generation of fitness enthusiast. Each fitness brand has created a culture to draw a niche customer.

In the same way, each church develops its own culture. Every denomination or faith tribe has its own beliefs, practices, and behaviors. Culture is influenced by clergy, staff, leadership, and style of worship. A church's unique expression of faith gives it stability, a source of identity, and a competitive advantage. Leadership who have a teachable attitude evolve their church structures and processes over time. The alternative becomes a stale, entrenched culture that fails to draw young people, enjoy new converts, or engage its community in ministry. Churches develop a culture, and that culture impacts their results.

Jesus had much to say about the condition of seven churches in the book of Revelation. He gives a commendation, a complaint, and a command to five ekklesias, which provide information about the culture, lifestyle, and organizational construct of each individual believing community. Dr. J. Vernon McGee says, "There is a message for your church and a message for you personally in Jesus's message for each church."[3]

The accompanying charts may help simplify and summarize our discussion of these churches. Smyrna and Philadelphia, the two New Testament Revelation churches that Jesus commended without complaint, will be discussed later in this chapter. The following chart summarizes the dysfunctional condition of the remaining five New Testament Revelation churches. The chart depicts Jesus's commendation, complaint, and command for each of these churches:

Church	Commendation	Complaint	Command
Ephesus Rev. 2:1-7	Hard work and patient endurance	Loveless	Repent and do the work as you did at first
Pergamum Rev. 2:12-17	Loyal & keeps his name	Worldly	Repent
Thyatira Rev. 2:18-29	Works, love, faith, service, endurance, improvement	Idolatry	Repent
Sardis Rev. 3:1-6	Some keep faith	Dead	Wake up! Strengthen what little remains
Laodicea Rev. 3:14-22	None	Lukewarm	Turn from indifference and repent

Revelation Church

The word for church, *ekklesia*, is mentioned nineteen times before chapter 4 of Revelation. Each church is discussed according to the city where it is located, and together they represent a composite picture of the Church. This panoramic view extends from Pentecost, with an apostolic church, to *Parousia* (the second coming of Christ), with an apostate church over seven distinct periods of church history. The commendation that Jesus gives to four of these five churches is meant to affirm and encourage the fully committed members of the believing community. The Greek word *kaleo* means "to call," and *ek* means "out of." Therefore "ekklesia" is a group of people called out of the world for the purpose of making disciples for Jesus Christ. He is complimenting the teamwork and function of the healthiest aspects of each community, such as the Ephesians' hard work and the Thyatiran church's endurance.

Clinical Archetypes of Dysfunctional Church Cultures

Facility	Focus	Complaint	Spirituality	Existence	Attracts	Heart
Corporate	Power & Institution	Loveless	Compassionate	Off & On	Institutional	Asynchronous
Collegiate	Principles & Tradition	Worldly	Conspicuous	Enlightened	Judgmental	Swollen
Civic Club	Purpose & Pleasures	Wrong Doctrine	Counterfeit	Superficial	Empty	Dilated
City Council	Position & Politics	Dead	Compromising	Conflict	Selfish	Thickened
Country Club	Possessions & Wealth	Lukewarm	Complacent	Indifferent	Notional	Hard

Jesus's complaint to five of the seven churches is directed at the unfit members, and the leaders bear responsibility for allowing and not managing the behaviors, beliefs, and practices of their churches. The complaints are instructive and insightful to the organizational culture and limitations of many believing bodies. Jesus's command for each church is directed at the entire assembly, especially the leadership! An ekklesia who wants to get well will ask the same question as the apostle Paul: "Who will rescue me from this body of death?"[4]

There are many excellent discussions available on this passage of Scripture, but few make application from an organizational perspective. Church leaders could benefit more from this passage if they could apply these principles to their own churches. The next table is a more clinical depiction of the culture within each New Testament church. In addition to the Word, and information from history about geography, I used culture and sociology scholarship to extrapolate distinct archetypes from each unhealthy church that Jesus brought a complaint against. I've given each church an archetype name based on the forms these problems sometimes take today. Though the archetypes are arbitrary, the Word of God to each church is not, and therefore has clinical relevance to the body of Christ in present-day assemblies. The last column of the chart gives a summary depiction of the essence of each archetype and of the pathology that would develop within the heart of each ekklesia from exposure to their particular diseased condition. Regardless of the specific cause of heart failure, the heart of each ekklesia becomes dysfunctional to Jesus and the Kingdom.

The Corporate Church (Ephesus)[5] – Boardroom leadership and volunteer Christians

Ephesus was an established harbor city with a large population relative to other cities in the region. Its location in Asia Minor placed it at the intersection of major trade routes. It was a gateway to Greece for visitors from all directions. The apostle Paul started the church of Ephesus; therefore, it is known as an apostolic church. He used it as a center for evangelism for about three years while

21

it flourished. Jesus commended the committed Christians in Ephesus saying, "I know your deeds, your hard work and your perseverance."[6] The church grew in power, and the institution that Paul established eventually became more concerned about their importance than about their original mission to spread the gospel and to love each other. They had a tendency to herald the logo of their institution more than the Kingdom of God. Jesus told them, "Yet I hold this against you: You have forsaken the love you had at first."[7] This believing community focused more on establishing power and building up their institution than on loving Jesus and other people.

Jesus basically complained that they were cold and lacked love. What good is a compassionless spirituality? Even nonbelievers perform deeds and good works! Many of our churches grow in stature until they become corporations that make financial and labor demands on their members without developing disciples with a love for Jesus.

Having lost their love for Jesus and other people, the community at Ephesus became selfish, mainly building up their own church, not the Kingdom. Leadership functioned more like the boardroom of a corporation, whereby executive members dole out decisions based upon organizational goals, without the will of God. Members serve as volunteer-employees whose primary goal is to carry out the functions of the church. They are indifferent to the needs of people around them.

These churches attract and value people who like working in the institution for the fulfillment it gives them rather than serving Jesus with their spiritual gifts according to his will. God never removed his presence from the Ephesian church,[8] but he did take away his power and blessing. Their hearts beat asynchronously because of their double-minded nature. Jesus charged them to, "Repent and do the things you did at first."[9] He wanted them to turn their hearts away from themselves and toward him.

The Collegiate Church (Pergamum)[10] – Tenure leadership and Sunday Christians

Pergamum was the capital of its Roman province. It was heralded as a center of learning, especially in medicine and religion. The city boasted one of the first city libraries, which was massive in scale and contained many manuscripts and books. A set of scrolls would be an easily recognizable symbol of this community that placed such an emphasis on intellectual pursuit. Jesus commended the church for holding fast despite having to exist where "Satan has his throne." In fact, Jesus says, "Yet you remain true to my name. You did not renounce your faith in me."[11] Loyalty to any friend, especially Jesus, is a worthy trait.

These learned believers were worldly. They upheld the teachings of Balaam, who enticed the Israelites to sin by eating food sacrificed to idols, and of the Nicolaitans, a heretical sect that taught spiritual liberty to practice idolatry and immorality. In the ivory tower of the intellectual, Pergamum believers focused on the principles of a doctrine and tradition of their design that endorsed Jesus, but they did not act out his love. Clearly, there is a difference between knowing Christian doctrine intellectually and knowing it sympathetically.

They arrogantly lived out a conspicuous Christianity evidenced by faith without works. Their church was more like a faculty lounge that only attracted people who wanted to be "enlightened" by a religion that accepted worldly principles. They preached tolerance but tended to be judgmental of others who had opinions or behaviors that differed from their own. Their hearts swelled in dysfunction as they became more enlightened. The apostle Timothy wrote about the harmful effect of doctrinal issues on believers:[12]

> If anyone teaches otherwise (false doctrines) and does not agree to the
> sound instruction of our Lord Jesus Christ and to godly teaching, they
> are conceited and understand nothing. They have an unhealthy interest
> in controversies and quarrels about words that result in envy, strife,
> malicious talk, evil suspicions and constant friction between men of

corrupt mind, who have been robbed of the truth and who think that godliness is a means to financial (personal) gain.

The pride of intellectualism leads many to believe that they are smarter than God—or at least a god themselves. The believers at Pergamum placed their interpretations and beliefs above everyone else, leading God to complain about their worldly nature. Paul asks, "Has not God made foolish the wisdom of the world?"[13] "For it is written: 'I will destroy the wisdom of the wise; the intelligence of the intelligent I will frustrate.' "[14] Their hearts were as visibly swollen as their opinions, but both were inaccurate and out of step with the nature of the Spirit.

This collegial atmosphere creates Sunday Christians. Members parade in well-pressed garments on Sunday but are nowhere to be found thereafter. Leadership belongs to the tenured members who enjoy the pomp and circumstance of ornamental robes and self-importance. Rank trumps spiritual authority.

The Civic Club Church (Thyatira)[15] – Fraternity leadership and fun Christians

Thyatira was a small inland town in Asia Minor. The town developed into a business and networking center because of its location and people. The businesswoman Lydia, the seller of purple, lived in Thyatira.[16] Connections between people were definitely interrelated within the business community. Jesus had many words of commendation for the church of Thyatira: "I know your deeds, your love and faith, your service and perseverance, and that you are now doing more than you did at first."[17] The church was functioning more like a civic club than a church. They were devoted to a mission that was not of the gospel.

The believers of Ephesus had only works, and the believers of Pergamum had only faith, but the believers of Thyatira demonstrated a little of both. Jesus's complaint was that they had tolerance for immoral behavior. "You tolerate that woman Jezebel, who calls herself a prophet. By her teaching she misleads my servants into sexual immorality and the eating of food sacrificed to idols. I have given her time to repent of her immorality, but she is unwilling. So I will cast her on a bed of suffering, and I will make those who commit adultery with her suffer intensely, unless they repent of her ways."[18]

Like any good civic club, they focused on their purpose of serving people. However, this passage suggests that their leadership tolerated a lifestyle of pleasure-seeking and even immoral behavior. They were fun Christians who were indifferent to the real needs in their community! The Thyatira believers were impure and lacked morality. God's beloved children can't worship him with an offensive and unfit lifestyle.

This believing community demonstrated a counterfeit spirituality. Their performance seemed authentic on the surface, but they lacked substance. They had a fake dilated heart. They had a "mild case of orthodox religion grafted onto a heart that is sold out to the world in its pleasures and its tastes and ambitions."[19] This community attracted shallow people who were only committed to the brand of the Greek lexicon that symbolically represented their social club and its lifestyle of good deeds and recreation against the backdrop of immorality.

The City Council Church (Sardis)[20] – Political leadership and dead Christians

Sardis was an old, established, inland city located on a plateau, where trade and commerce were practiced. City leaders were heavily involved in politics. One's position influenced his ability to be successful, and this hierarchical attitude negatively affected the spiritual atmosphere. An appropriate symbol for this community would be a set of scales where they measured themselves to be greater than the Holy Spirit. Jesus could only commend the fact that some had kept the faith. They had very little positive for him to compliment. Instead, Jesus said, "I know your deeds; you have a reputation of being alive, but you are dead. Wake up! Strengthen what remains and is about to die, for I have found your deeds unfinished in the sight of my God."[21] I want to hear the words "well done my faithful servant." I don't want to be told that I'm dead! The reason for his strong condemnation is that the believers of Sardis were manipulative and infected with a lack of conviction, faith, and belief.

These believers narcissistically focused on their social positions and on politics, offering only a compromising spirituality to God. Leaders acted more like officials in a city council or congressional chamber who ruled politically over others with a dense heart. The Holy Spirit had been so neglected and disobeyed that he was asleep and absent. The people of Sardis were like so many in our dead churches. They replaced the Spirit of God with their own self-righteous spirit, and repelled all who were holy including the clergy.

Every one of these churches had a hopeful remnant of faithful believers who were stunted from a life of intimacy with Christ, because they let social church relationships prevent them from creating another healthy ekklesia. Satan worked through the self-serving members to consume righteousness, leaving the by-product of conflict and a quenched Spirit.

The Country Club Church (Laodicea)[22] – Golf course leadership and comfortable Christians

Laodicea was located inland on a fertile plain. It was a bedroom community of Colossae, which was only eleven miles away. Like many cities of that time, it was on a major trade route. Laodicea developed into a banking center where an extensive textile industry contributed to the region's financial wealth. The apostle Epaphras started the church.[23] One of its most famous citizens was Cicero. Possessions and wealth were important to the people there. Laodicea was a community where the wealthiest citizens lived and worked. Its major weakness was its lack of an adequate water supply.

This was the only church that Jesus did not commend. He had nothing good to say to the believers of Laodicea. They were known as the apostate church because Jesus said, "You are neither cold nor hot. I wish you were either one or the other! So, because you are lukewarm—neither hot nor cold—I am about to spit you out of my mouth. You say, 'I am rich; I have acquired wealth and do not need a thing.' But you do not realize that you are wretched, pitiful, poor, blind and naked."[24]

I live in Augusta, Georgia, a well-known golf community. The symbol of the Augusta National Golf Club, home of the Masters Golf Tournament, is internationally recognized. Golf is an enjoyable pastime, but it is associated with the affluent. Many of the Laodiceans were affluent too. As such, an appropriate symbol for the people of Laodicea would be a country club logo.

Jesus's complaint was that they were lukewarm. They practiced a useless, complacent spirituality. They were "comfortable Christians," unconcerned with others' needs while smugly focusing on their own achievements and pleasures. The Laodicean community represented the worst among believers—they existed without any needs because they already had everything they needed. These believers demonstrated no faith and no works. Today, similar churches live a country-club existence, appealing only to other indifferent affluent people. Leadership decisions are made on their golf courses. Their hard heart is unavailable to the Holy Spirit and therefore not teachable. The apostle Timothy addressed the condition of a hard heart:[25]

> Command those who are rich in this present world not to be arrogant nor to put their hope in wealth, which is so uncertain, but to put their hope in God, who richly provides us with everything for our enjoyment. Command them to do good, to be rich in good deeds, and to be generous and willing to share. In this way they will lay up treasure for themselves as a firm foundation for the coming age, so that they may take hold of the life that is truly life.

A.W. Tozer said:

> A look into history will quickly convince any interested person that the true church has almost always suffered more from prosperity than from poverty. The average church has so established itself organizationally and financially that God is simply not necessary to it. So entrenched is its

authority and so stable are the religious habits of its members that God could withdraw Himself completely from it as it could run on for years on its own momentum.[26]

Do you now or have you ever attended a church that sounded like one of the clinical archetypes above? A faltering church probably displays more than one archetype. Churches are organic entities filled with a mixture of fit and unfit followers. Some members are vital Christ followers, and some are dead to the Kingdom. It is more likely that a combination of archetypes is active at any given church. Jesus was giving an important warning to those New Testament churches, and his warnings are applicable today. The core values, beliefs, and practices of a church reside in its heart. The mouthpiece, hands, and behavior of an assembly reflect the condition of its heart, but the heart is not the cause of dysfunction. Rather, the physical condition of the heart is a consequence of deeper pathology within the community. The Revelation churches that Christ condemned each demonstrate a particular type of dysfunctional heart common among faltering churches today.

The heart's pathology is only important insofar as it gives a clue as to the underlying problem. Notice that despite the specific and differing heart pathology within each Revelation church that Christ condemned, every heart is equally dysfunctional. David expresses the consequences of a dysfunctional heart on his body: "I am poured out like water, and all my bones are out of joint. My heart has turned to wax; it has melted within me."[27] The Bible uses the term stony or *eben* in Greek to classify the dysfunctional heart, regardless of the cause.[28] A stony heart is cold and hard. It is not pliable or teachable. It functions only to serve itself, not Christ. A dysfunctional heart cannot invite the Spirit of God.

Unfortunately, much of the discussion about a changed heart for churches has evolved into semantics surrounding the terms "restoration," "transformation," or "revolution." There has been little emphasis from our church leaders on developing a healthy spiritual heart or culture. Understanding the heart's ailment is only important if treatment is desired. Otherwise, a poorly functioning heart prevents the love of Christ from flowing to the members of the body.

Fit Church Culture

Among the laurel trees and vineyards on the rolling hills along Greece's Cogamis River lies a picturesque valley where early believers received the greatest commendation from the Lord Jesus Christ.[29] Alluvial soil, excellent wine, and beauty attracted Greeks to the Anatolian countryside where a "little Athens" served as an isolated fortress city. It was named Philadelphia because of the love Attalus II had for his brother Eumenes, the king of Pergamum. These early Christians were known for their devotion to the Word of God and for their works: two attributes of a fit church. The early assembly at Philadelphia was only one of two believing communities out of seven that did not receive condemnation from Jesus Christ in the vision of John in Revelation.

The other ekklesia was at Smyrna, a beautiful harbor town where Anatolians erected beast-like statues to their gods and Greeks adorned the city with many temples to their gods: Zeus, Diana, Aphrodite, Apollo, and Asclepius. Smyrna means "myrrh" or "suffering," and suffering is what this believing community had to endure. First of all, believers at Smyrna were poor in material resources and money. In fact, Jesus says, "I know thy works, and tribulation, and poverty, (but thou art rich)."[30] Believers gave everything they had to the early church, but Jesus knew of their spiritual wealth. He commended them for their steadfastness and faithfulness. Their poverty represents a limitation from an external circumstance. In addition to their poverty, they suffered persecution and were martyred.

Persecution represents one of many external circumstances that can limit churches. Today we hear of Egyptian Coptic churches being bombed or Christians in the Middle East being martyred. In the United States, persecution of believers is mild but increasing as compared to New Testament times. Imagine how committed early followers must have been to function so successfully in their environments of persecution. In AD 155, Polycarp, Bishop of Smyrna, was burned alive in the local stadium. *Foxe's Book of Martyrs* identifies five million believers who died for Christ during this period. Despite the limitations of poverty and persecution, the believers of Smyrna remained faithful until the end.[31]

Believers in Philadelphia faced their own challenges. In addition to occasional warfare, the region suffered many earthquakes like the "great earthquake" in AD 17 that totally destroyed the city. Cracks in the infrastructure, soil erosion, and occasional tremors served as constant reminders of their brittle existence, but these were insignificant compared to the persecution they had to endure from both governing and religious authorities. Jewish subjects paid an annual tax to legally exempt them from worship of the emperor. Gentiles and Jewish believers of Jesus were not welcome in the Jewish synagogue; therefore, they were subject to the empire's pagan demands. They were forced to denounce Jesus Christ and instead publicly, socially, and religiously worship the emperor. They experienced intense periods of persecution at the hands of Roman emperors such as: Nero from 64 to 68 (Paul was beheaded); Domitian from 81-96 (John was exiled); Trajan from 104 to 117 (Ignatius was burned at the stake); Marcus Aurelius from 161 to 180 (Polycarp was martyred); Severus from 200 to 211; Maximinius from 235 to 237; Decius from 250 to 253; Valerian from 257 to 260; Aurelian from 270 to 275; and, the worst of all, Diocletian from 303 to 313. Diocletian rescinded Christian legal rights and required them to make sacrifices to Roman gods.

Early believers lived under serious daily pressure to deny their Lord and to participate in either Judaism or in the religious aspects of the imperial cult. Daily persecution limited their freedom to practice and to share the gospel message, but their commitment to the Lord won them commendation from Jesus, despite their obstacles. As a result, Philadelphia also became known as the live church, the believing church, or the Bible-believing church.[32] Of the seven churches mentioned in Revelation, only Philadelphia and Smyrna are credited as continuously existing until the modern era.[33]

You may be asking: Why am I getting a history lesson? I want to demonstrate what an optimally fit believing community is all about—Jesus! It's not about structures, staffing, programs, numbers, or excuses. It's about the Word and service to the Lord. These two churches did not receive criticism, only praise. Let's see why in Revelation.

> I know your deeds. See, I have placed before you an open door that no one can shut. I know that you have little strength, yet you have kept my word and have not denied my name.... Since you have kept my command to endure patiently, I will also keep you from the hour of trial that is going to come on the whole world to test the inhabitants of the earth.[34]

Their deeds were their works. They were exercising their spiritual muscles by performing ministry among believers and mission among nonbelievers. Believing communities are created in Christ Jesus, his workmanship, to do his will.[35] Their faith produced the fruit of works! As James says, "show me your faith without works, and I will show you my faith by my works."[36] Saving faith produces deeds. Jesus praised their work of spreading the gospel.

The open door probably refers to the knowledge of the Scriptures. The Philadelphians are commended for keeping his Word and being a Bible-believing church. This church planted the Word of God in the world and lasted longer than the other churches. They were fit because they reproduced the God-breathed knowledge of the gospel of Jesus Christ into the DNA of subsequent generations from that one location until almost the thirteenth century. Credited as sending missionaries to start the Christian church in India, Philadelphia has long been known as "the missionary church."[37] During the Crusades, Christians and Saracens fought in Philadelphia, but more recently Greeks and Turks fought in this Turkish town, which is known as Alaşehir today. Christians continuously inhabited this region well into the twelfth century, until Seljuk Turks brutally removed every vestige of the old civilization. Only a few pillars remain today.

Can your church last that long? Will your church be a viable believing community for your grandchildren? Are you creating disciples of Christ for the next generation?

In Greek, the word "strength" can be translated as *dunamin*, the word for dynamite. God provides just enough power for his children to accomplish his tasks. Our faith provides power,[38] and the Holy Spirit gives us power as well.[39] The Philadelphian believing community had just enough strength to keep his Word and not deny the precious name of Jesus. Unto persecution and death, this committed band of believers remained disciplined, abstained from cultural deterrents, and acknowledged the name of Jesus Christ, the name to which every knee will bow upon, above and below the earth.[40] In addition, Jesus lastly commended this fit church for keeping a patient watch for his return. Like the bride who waits for her groom, this ekklesia was living out the attitude of holy expectation for the one she loved.

The Philadelphian and Smyrnan believers did not have any denominational affiliations, but they represent a composite picture of a fit church. This message is meant for believers and churches as much today as two thousand years ago. These two churches mentioned in Revelation exemplify the heart of Christ and the pursuit of fit Christian living.

A look at the Thessalonian church reveals yet another example of an optimally fit believing community, which has the same ingredients as those of Philadelphia and Smyrna. The apostle Paul spent only three Sabbaths in Thessalonica during his second missionary journey, but the gospel came to the people in Word, in power, and in the Holy Spirit.[41] This church was a testimony to all of Greece, Macedonia, and Achaia, and was an example to the Corinthians.[42] After Timothy reported the faith and the love of the Thessalonians,[43] Paul wrote his first epistle and first letter to this believing community. J. Vernon McGee says the letter has a threefold purpose: "to confirm young converts in the elementary truth of the gospel, to condition them to go on unto holy living, and to comfort them regarding the return of Christ."[44]

Acts 17 chronicles the ministry of Paul to the Thessalonians, and his letter to their ekklesia reveals the same ingredients the Philadelphian and Smyrna Revelation churches had. The spiritual ekklesia within these churches displays the ingredients of a fit church culture:

Saved – single-minded focus
Suffering – dying dedication
Second-coming attitude – patiently waits

Steadfast – true to the Word of God
Surrendered – intimately connected
Submitted – the fruit of works

Soul-winning – coordinated use of spiritual muscles
Served – despite significant limitations
Succession-minded – sharing the gospel unto the next generation

Ingredients of a Fit Church Culture

By using the same format used for the dysfunctional Revelation churches, the clinical expression of a fit church culture can be summarized in the following table as the fit church archetype.

Facility	Focus	Complaint	Spirituality	Existence	Attracts	Heart
f✝s	Next Generation	None	Christ-Centered	Committed to Christ	Followers	Conditioned for Christ

Fit Church Archetype

33

My descriptors for the fit church are "Father's holy sanctuary" and "follower training site," or f✝s (the letter "t" represents the cross for the word "Holy" and the word "training"). This designation serves two purposes. First, f✝s demonstrates the intimate relationship between the Holy Spirit and the church body who reverently worships and seeks to know Jesus in the church, a holy place or sanctuary. These assemblies exemplify their healthy culture by living the fitness ingredients described above. In a healthy church culture, God's people conform to the Lord. Second, a fit culture is one that produces followers.

In the Bible, the apostle Paul fondly uses athletic imagery to describe the Christian life. (See 1 Corinthians 9:24-27, 1 Timothy 6:12, 2 Timothy 4:7-8, and Hebrews 12:1.) The author of Hebrews, probably Paul, compares our spiritual life to an athletic contest, where followers must train to develop the perseverance and endurance to run the race.[45] A fit church becomes a type of follower training site, a vehicle that fulfills its purpose by working in community and in the world to reproduce fit followers so that the church can accomplish its unique vision. Our conduct should be worthy of our calling,[46] worthy of the gospel,[47] and worthy of the Lord.[48] Believers who are training to become worthy followers enjoy the Lord's rest and refreshing.

We know that a fit church is a holy sanctuary and spiritual fitness center, but how does a church change its culture to become an f✝s? The first step is to recognize the difference between the things that need to be changed versus the things that cannot be changed. A five-foot athlete who loves to play basketball cannot change his height. Therefore, he may not be a professional basketball player. His desire to be around the game could motivate him to pursue a career in some other aspect of basketball.

Churches similarly must recognize their limitations. A rural church may not have the population to support an extensive music ministry or youth program, and it may not produce an abundance of new local converts. Though limited, this rural church should still adopt a vision and mission to perform at an optimal level. Some churches like the Revelation churches Smyrna and Philadelphia have significant limitations (size, location, poverty, resources), but they've found a way to serve God, to follow his Word, and to keep his commands. These churches demonstrate optimal fitness because they persevere, serving and loving their Lord despite political, sociological, and religious pressures.[49] Churches that have hierarchal, institutional, or ministerial limitations are not exempt from participating fully in the Kingdom. Every church has some type of limitation. Each church must acknowledge their limitations and develop a vision appropriate for their ekklesia.

Leadership should develop the Mind of Christ for their ekklesia by working through their strengths and opportunities, not their limitations. To have a vision, mission, and purpose for their church, leaders will build unity and the Mind of Christ. Decision making that aligns with the goals above creates health and changes church culture. (The Mind of Christ will be discussed in more detail in the chapter called "The Wellness Toolbox.")

A church culture that is internally branded to its congregants and externally branded to the local community can build enthusiasm among participants who become excited over the church's direction and purpose. Folks who don't buy in to the vision and culture may become "leavers". This has been shown to be an important factor in growing churches, because it reduces free ridership and increases member commitment and growth.[50]

Fitness Spectrum

After I learned about organizational behavior, branding, and performance, I applied that knowledge to improving medical practices and churches. The experience taught me that there are different degrees of health among organizations. When Jesus discussed the seven New Testament churches, he also gave a qualitative assessment of their cultures. Like people, church culture can be categorized by its level of fitness. No single measurement can accurately describe the culture or condition of a church.

Since the primary audience of this book is church leaders, please do not take personal offense to this terminology or the level of fitness within your church's body. It does not necessarily reflect on the spiritual condition of individual members. Body fitness is an organizational construct. As a mature Christian and leader, be open to the Holy Spirit helping you to discern your church's level of fitness. Then follow the steps to making the personal and organizational changes that will contribute to elevating your body's fitness level. This nomenclature is not intended for judgement. It primarily describes specific inputs (afflictions, conflict, leadership, fitness ingredients) and outputs (enthusiasts, followers, productivity, energy). The fitness spectrum can be a tool to help leaders improve their church's culture. After having studied churches over a long period of time, I can place churches into the following spectrum of organizational fitness: nominal, languid, well, and fit. A chart of this spectrum follows.

CONDITION	NOMINAL	LANGUID	WELL	FIT
Afflictions	many	some	managed	controlled
Conflict	+/-	++	+	-
Followers	+/-	+	++	+++
Enthusiasts	+/-	+	E	E^2
Driver, $f =$ (function of)	controllers	leaders	processes	followers
Output	+/-	X	10X	100X
Energy	+/-	inward	outward	upward
Fitness Ingredients	+/-	some	most	all

Church Fitness Spectrum

Nominal means existing in name only.[51] Some churches are nominal within the Kingdom. As a church, they embody the love and value as the bride of Christ.

But as an assembly, they have lost their love of the Lord. They are selfish, have little faith, and have turned away from the Lord. These churches have a history of conventional structures that haven't been adjusted for some time. This archetype develops few followers, fewer enthusiasts, and many afflictions. Their remnant of followers may exhibit some faith or works. Nominal churches have many similarities to the churches at Sardis and Laodicea in Revelation. Jesus called them lukewarm or dead. The members are not dead to each other; they are dead to Christ. This church archetype lacks energy—the power of the Holy Spirit. The spiritual ingredients found within healthy churches may not be found in nominal churches.

The primary driver of the nominal church is a function of controlling leadership called "controllers." These are leaders who are more interested in having their own way in disputed matters than in following the way of the gospel of Jesus Christ. Organizationally, very few of these church leaders reflect the Mind of Christ (vision, mission, purpose, and behavior). Conflict is minimal because few members argue for the gospel. Leaders tend to have hardened, dysfunctional hearts. They quench the Holy Spirit. The apostle Paul says that they live as enemies of the cross and their minds are on earthly things.[52]

Nominal churches tend to have declining memberships. Among mainline Protestant churches, their worship attendance to member ratio is less than 0.37. These churches have few visitors. New members tend to be "switchers" (believers who move from one church to another) who are just like the church members that they join. The church becomes a comfortable place that many treat like a social or civic club in which to practice a comfortable or convenient Christianity. Leadership limits the culture of the nominal church. They tend to be consumed with maintaining or preserving the church, not with developing a Christ-centered strategy of service.

Languid churches, churches that lack energy or enthusiasm, probably make up the largest category within the fitness spectrum. Many aspects of a languid church are healthy, and they tend to be rooted in the gospel, but they are more like the remaining Revelation churches that Christ condemned. Languid also refers to an unwillingness or inability to exert oneself due to fatigue, physical weakness, or disease. In churches, sin, selfishness, and suffering can zap a congregation of its energy and quench the Holy Spirit.

Jesus complained that these churches were loveless, worldly, or functioned with wrong doctrine. They had a dysfunctional heart that was out of sync, swollen, or dilated. These churches had inconsistent faith and works. Size and location are not specific to this archetype.

These types of churches tend to face both afflictions and conflicts, which cause their weakness or fatigue, but they lack the skill or processes to manage them very well. Too much energy is directed inward, to control the newest affliction, rather than outward, to build the Kingdom. Attenders tend to be unattached and intermittent. Congregants worship and participate as they please. The behavior of these members puts into question the integrity of the church's belief system. Languid churches tend to have the highest abundance of free-riding membership (members who attend but do not give or participate).

Languid churches are very dependent on their leadership. They tend to be limited by their ordained and or non-ordained leadership. They lack visionary leaders. Their fitness condition can fall to nominal or rise to wellness-oriented. These churches have the potential to get either healthier or sicker. Most leaders lack the organizational skills, strategies, and processes to build up fit followers who become enthusiastic about serving in the church. Structures are lacking to systematically mature and disciple followers into fit, enthusiastic believers.

The health of languid churches comes from the remnant of members who are fit followers. Whereas nominal churches have no spiritual productivity, languid churches have a measurable output in building and planting, or an amount called X. Some enthusiasts exist, and they are responsible for the viable programs and ministries. Languid churches exhibit some of the fitness ingredients that we've discussed. Attendance at worship, membership trends, or mission participation of languid churches can be stable, in decline, or growing slightly. Membership rolls may swell because they do not remove the "leavers" or "switchers", but languid churches have the lowest worship attendance to member ratios.

Well churches are wellness-oriented and have leadership submitted to Jesus whose primary purpose is to build up fit followers. Leadership uses the Mind of Christ to communicate to the body about their purpose, mission, goals, etc. Ordained and non-ordained leadership serve together as co-leaders to accomplish the vision of their church. Structures are in place to manage afflictions, people, and important processes. Leaders encourage the beliefs and behaviors of their members through scriptural teaching and correction. They exhibit both faith and works.

These churches demonstrate most of the ingredients found in the fit church archetype. Afflictions are few, and followers are many. Conflicts are managed continually without difficulty. Well churches turn their energy outward with the use of their abundant enthusiasts, or E. Output can be measured as 10X. Healthy processes lead to fit churches. Strategy and processes have been developed to reproduce fit followers who fulfill the vision, mission, and purpose of the ekklesia. These churches are universally growing. Interestingly, well churches have higher member turnover. Well churches are devoted to the Mind of Christ (unified vision, mission, purpose, and behavior) for their ekklesia. As new members learn more about their church's vision, mission, and purpose, they either embrace them or leave. Well churches have fewer lukewarm members.

Fit churches can be large or small. They contain all the characteristics of well churches, plus they are optimally fit and programmed to pass on the gospel of Jesus Christ to the next generation, despite their own limitations. They respond to afflictions and conflict in healthy ways. Fit churches exhibit the traits of fit New Testament churches like Smyrna, Philadelphia, and Thessalonica. Their energy is directed upward toward God. Fit churches have a culture that encourages and produces followers and enthusiasts. If wellness-oriented churches have enthusiasts, or E, then fit churches have multiples of enthusiasts, or E^2. They function organizationally like a follower fitness center.

The driver for fit churches is its followers who are wholly devoted to spreading the gospel and strengthening the Church. Leadership understands the important drivers for fitness, and evangelism is their primary goal. Their focus is outward as they aim to love others not only in the church, but also in the community. Fit churches bear the fruit of new believers because of their worthy followers. They have removed themselves as the focus and instead serve to maintain the processes that keep the church running the race. They press onward toward the goal of spreading the gospel.[53]

The following diagram demonstrates the fluidity between each level of fitness, and the conditions necessary to move from one level to another.

	Heart		Mind		Body		Hands	
Nominal	←→	Languid	←→	Well	←→	Fit	←→	Optimally Fit
	Change heart		Leadership Ed		Planting		Followership	

Changing Levels on the Church Fitness Spectrum

The far left side shows the nominal church, and the far right side shows the optimally fit church. Depending upon the internal or external forces acting upon a church at any point in time, movement can be bidirectional in the diagram. For example, if there is a change in ordained or non-ordained leadership, so that the Holy Spirit is quenched through conflict, disunity, or disease, then a church could decline from being a well church to being a languid church.

The words above and between each church category in the diagram describe the leadership changes that must be made in order to ascend or descend to the next level of fitness. The series of prescriptions at the end of each chapter is designed to accelerate leadership transformation and aid in this process. The mechanisms by which that change occurs are below and between each church category. The following chapters will provide the understanding and tools to make these important changes, and the fitness exercises in Appendix 4 will supplement the process. For example, elevating from a nominal church to a languid church requires a change in the heart of leadership. Languid churches need to develop the Mind of Christ (which we'll discuss in detail later) through leadership education. By creating the processes, the culture, and a follower training site, the Body can become well. If well churches want to become fit churches, the Body must orient itself toward Kingdom building and planting new churches. Fit churches can climb to the highest elevation, optimal fitness, by using their followers despite limitations.

To change trajectory, nominal churches need to recognize their afflictions, and leadership must want to get well. The prescriptions set forth in this book provide the antidote for nominal church leaders to develop their faith and build the ingredients of a healthy church. Ascending to the next level of fitness is dependent upon a changed heart among leaders, which requires understanding church health, healthy archetypes, and church disease. Nominal churches need both personal and corporate repentance. The primary goal is for leaders to submit to downward growth, putting new roots down. The primary focus should be to draw nourishment from and to grow in Christ by placing a renewed emphasis on reading and studying the Word.[54] Becoming secure and firm in our beliefs prevents false teachers and the world from shaking our faith.

To ascend to the next level of fitness, languid churches must grow their branches upward in the grace and gifts of the Holy Spirit. Leaders must have a teachable attitude. Education of leaders should be the church's primary purpose. If leadership can clarify the Mind of Christ and make use of the wellness drivers, then necessary organizational systems can be developed. Improvement depends upon creating a follower training site, or fts, a corporate process whereby members continue to develop and train as worthy followers.

Well churches can ascend to a fit church level if leaders focus inward upon the Body to discern the appropriate Kingdom-building strategy for its pipeline of fit followers who want to exercise the virtues of Christ and holy living. Leadership should begin to discuss strategies on how God would have them multiply within the Kingdom. When a church is optimally fit, then it will "worship the Lord in the beauty of holiness"[55] and pass on their Christian heritage to the next generation of followers.[56]

Fitness oriented churches are already building and planting within the Kingdom. If the fit Body can function without the limitations of their external or internal circumstances, then they can ascend to the rare level of the optimally fit church. Jesus would commend this church and say, "Well done." The reward for this Body is seeing the Savior again, being able to present the young converts of their ministries to Christ, and letting them share in the glory of his advent.[57] Their motto is "to live is Christ, to live is fruitful labor."[58] The following chart summarizes the steps that are necessary to summit the fitness spectrum. Under the heading condition, Rx, is the treatment necessary for each row.

CONDITION	NOMINAL	LANGUID	WELL	FIT
Rx Purpose	new heart	leadership	body	others
Rx Key	repentance	teachability	f✝s	followers
Rx Focus	downward	upward	inward	outward
Rx Goal	leader educ.	*BUFF	**WIN	multiply
Growth	root in Christ	grace & gifts	holy living	loving others

Steps for Improving Church Fitness
*Build Up Fit Followers, **Win others to Christ

History has its own laws, and no institution escapes the ravages of time,
however holy and great its founder.
Carlo Caretto

Fitness Moment

- Church culture is important because the beliefs and behaviors of people guide their actions and practices.
- The Revelation churches give insight into healthy and unhealthy archetypes.
- As churches lose focus on Christ, they become secularized and begin to function like any combination of the unhealthy archetypes.
- Eventually the heart of a church changes to reflect its dysfunction.
- The churches of Smyrna, Philadelphia, and Thessalonica model the ingredients of a fit ekklesia.
- The archetype of a fit church builds faith through holiness, Christ-centeredness, and spreading the gospel via fit followers.
- Descriptors for church organizational health are "nominal," "languid," "wellness-oriented," and "fit."
- Churches may exhibit different levels of fitness over time.
- Specific measurable goals help leaders achieve the next level of fitness.
- Our prescription is to reflect on the condition of our own heart as well as the condition of our church.

Reflect

Sig: *follow the instructions*
Refill(s): *prn — as needed*
Comments: *No substitutions permitted*

Search me, God, and know my heart;
test me and know my anxious thoughts.
See if there is any offensive way in me,
and lead me in the way everlasting.[59]

Reflection plays a major role in the life of the nation of Israel. The Word has been passed along by an oral tradition that reflects on the Israelites' historical relationship with God. By retelling stories like the Passover, the Exodus, the Wilderness, the Captivity, and the rebuilding of the temple, Christians can learn from Israel's past experiences. New generations can make adjustments to strengthen their relationship with the Lord. The purpose of corporate reflection is to recognize that our assembly may be out of plumb with the will of God [60] and separated from optimal fitness (the life of God) because of a dysfunctional heart.[61] Like the great number of feeble, blind, and withered people gathered by the colonnade at Bethesda, our assembly may be perched on the edge of renewal, waiting for the water to stir while the real healer stands nearby.[62] Reflection allows the assembly to do more than look inward with a kind of longing hope. It gives people time to listen to the Great Physician.

Jesus wants to stop the perpetual cycle of paralysis and sickness within our churches. He knows that broken cisterns cannot hold his spring of living water[63] and that many ekklesias exercise their knowledge of divine healing through reason only. Like the paralytic our lack of faith or knowledge does not preclude us from being healed.

During reflection, the assembly must reevaluate their heart. Physicians listen to their patient's heart while the patient is sitting quietly. When I approach a newborn for his initial exam, my first contact is with my eyes searching over the baby looking for the proper color and perfusion. Next, I place my warmed hand on the chest over the baby's heart. I feel for the proper function of the heart. I notice if the heart moves normally under my hand. Finally, I listen to the sounds of the heart with a warmed stethoscope. I listen for the absence of silence between the two heart-sounds "Lub Dub Lub Dub" or, as Leonard Sweet says, "Do Be-Do, Do Be-Do".[64] I listen for anything that shouldn't be heard.

Positioning the instrument at various strategic places on the chest allows me to hear the whole heart. In newborns, frequent exams allow me to follow the baby's circulatory transition from life in the womb to life in the world. Similarly, God follows his children's transition from their second birth to mature obedience. He examines his church. A spirit of quietude in both the physician and the patient allows for optimal evaluation. The patient, too, observes, listens, and contemplates during the examination. Reflection is not for visitation, fellowship, or fun, but for contemplation in solitude with the leadership saying, "Search me, O God, know my heart."

The Physician performs his exam and helps the church understand the condition of her heart, but he speaks with a "gentle whisper" so the ekklesia must be attentive.[65] Jesus came to the man at Bethesda, and he will come to your assembly... if you want to be healed.

As you read and participate in this fitness journey, reflect on the condition of your heart and the condition of your church. Make notes as you are led.

3

UNDERSTANDING FITNESS

Therefore we do not lose heart.
Though outwardly we are wasting away,
yet inwardly we are being renewed day by day.
2 Corinthians 4:16

I was first exposed to the concept of fitness during physical education class in elementary school in 1966. President Lyndon B. Johnson created the Presidential Physical Fitness Award, stemming from the President's Youth Council on Fitness, which was originally started by Dwight D. Eisenhower ten years earlier.[1] All our teachers had bought into the idea, and they created an environment of competition, encouraging each of us to strive for this newly heralded award. I don't remember ever receiving the award, but I do remember trying my hardest at each exercise.

Brian, my thirty-one-year-old, athletic son, recently introduced me to a newer concept of fitness when he brought home a copy of *Men's Health* magazine.[2] We decided to replace our daily exercise routines with the *Men's Health* fitness tests, which also gave us a forum for togetherness. First, we measured seventy-five feet using a measuring tape, and placed orange soccer cones at each end. Next, we took turns timing our performance in running back and forth in order to accomplish three hundred yards, which was six laps. I had an exercise routine that included a combination of running, biking, and/or paddling, so I assumed that I would perform well. I went first. I completed four and a half of the six laps when Brian called, "TIME." He lasted for five and a half laps when I timed him. Yes, he beat his old dad, but even Brian fell short on the first of the twelve tests that determined optimal physical fitness. In all, I was measured to be fit in only one category and fell short of the mark in the others. I thought that I was fit, but this objective test suggested that I was not.

Churches have different fitness levels, and they can have health issues. Disease and injury can limit organizational fitness among churches. Old, established churches face different challenges than younger churches. Defining terms provides a better understanding of the fitness concept.

Definitions

What defines "fitness" in our spiritual lives or in our churches' lives? Theologians, academics, and many authors have written much about the concept of health, but very little about wellness or fitness. Various models, measures, or criterions have been offered, but most are found wanting and incomplete. Some thesauruses say "health," "wellness," and "fitness" are synonymous words. Before we begin building the model for church fitness, I want to "dig down deep and lay a foundation on rock."[3] Understanding the distinction between the terms health, wellness, and fitness helps us find the bedrock on which this model is built.

Many people and organizations try to explain the term "health." Though some have difficulty putting the term into words, most people know if they are generally "healthy" or not. Have you noticed that people seem to recognize (and perhaps comment on) the health of others? For example, in 1 Samuel, even

David's adversary, the Philistine Goliath "looked David over and saw that he was little more than a boy, glowing with health and handsome, and he despised him."[4] Do you sometimes despise the jogger, the cyclist or any otherwise fit person? Don't we all want, to some degree or another, to become more fit?

Health

Dictionary.com defines health as soundness of body or mind with freedom from disease or ailment.[5] The World Health Organization gives an expanded definition of health as "a state of complete physical, mental, and social well-being and not merely the absence of disease."[6] As a physician, I ascribe health to a more clinical and functional definition like the one found in *Merriam-Webster's Medical Dictionary*: "the condition of an organism with respect to the performance of its vital functions especially as evaluated subjectively or nonprofessionally."[7] The health of a person or organism like a church first has to be evaluated by that person or entity. When a patient reaches what he or she believes to be the threshold for abnormal function or dysfunction, then the patient believes their own health is compromised and often will seek professional help.

The point here is that the status of one's health begins as a *subjective* self-assessment of functionality. For some people, simply walking to their car and going to work reaches a baseline functional health; therefore, in their minds, they are "healthy." Other people have a higher bar for their health. They want to be able to exercise liberally and live pain-free in addition to simply attending to daily routines. This subjective difference in health perception among people and churches is important because it helps to explain why churches have different levels of motivation and urgency with respect to maintaining their own health. That's why it is important to have an external measure of health.

Members of the New Orleans Baptist Theological Seminary (NOBTS) have articulated one of the best comprehensive definitions of church health:

A healthy church is a church that seeks to obey the Great Commission and Great Commandments in its setting by being biblically based, spiritually dynamic, mission focused, servant led, and characterized by excellence in all that it does.[8]

Remember, the Great Commission states: "Then the eleven disciples went to Galilee, to the mountain where Jesus had told them to go. When they saw him, they worshiped him; but some doubted. Then Jesus came to them and said, 'All authority in heaven and on earth has been given to me. Therefore, go and make disciples of all nations, baptizing them in the name of the Father and of the Son and of the Holy Spirit, and teaching them to obey everything I have commanded you. And surely I am with you always, to the very end of the age.'"[9] The Great Commandment, on the other hand, was an answer to the question, "'Teacher, which is the greatest commandment in the Law?' Jesus replied: 'Love the Lord your God with all your heart and with all your soul and with all your mind.'"[10] Notice that the assignment is carried out within a specific context, but it is characterized by excellence as it is done with all of one's heart, soul, and mind.

The other descriptors used by the NOBTS—"biblically based," "spiritually dynamic," "mission focused," and "servant led"—are very important. These elements are the by-product of Jesus's life and as such should be incorporated into the Church. This type of definition of church health is important to the foundation of any church model.

Wellness

The term "wellness" addresses the point of ownership, taking responsibility for maintaining one's health. One medical dictionary defines wellness as the condition of good physical and mental health, especially when maintained by proper diet, exercise, and habits.[11] Again, Dictionary.com defines wellness "as the quality or state of being healthy in body and mind, especially as the result of deliberate effort."[12] In both definitions, work or diligence is required in order to maintain wellness, a higher standard of physical and mental health.

Another part of ownership is seeking advice from a professional health care provider or personal trainer. Such a relationship will help individuals function at their best and will help them create a culture and lifestyle of wellness.

Churches must understand that wellness takes energy and commitment. Church wellness is a lifestyle choice that leadership must demand and membership must adopt in order to promote a healthy culture. Wellness means that your church will invest the necessary resources to stem problems, train leaders, and monitor both staff and members. Wellness doesn't automatically happen; it's the result of proper attention to the Body (membership) and the Mind (Christ). We will discover more in our discussions of the Wellness Toolbox later.

Fitness

Finally, let's add another distinction to the trio of health, wellness, and fitness by defining the term "fitness." One dictionary defines fitness as "the state of being suitably adapted to an environment."[13] Another defines fitness as, "the capacity of an organism to survive and transmit its genotype to reproductively fertile offspring as compared to competing organisms."[14] Now we can see that fitness expands beyond the definition of wellness to involve not only the organism, but also how the organism survives in its environment and passes its traits on to the next generation.

For a church to exhibit wellness it must deliberately create a lifestyle focused on health. Fitness goes to another level. It reflects not only an existing church's wellness but also that church's ability to pass on that wellness to future generations. The church must nurture healthy offspring in order to pass along important ecclesiastical DNA. The gospel message about Jesus and the NOTBS definition represent a good summation of the church's DNA. Fitness is selfless because it imparts the genes of the ecclesiastical species for use in a new context to reach the next generation of believers.

In his book *11 Genetic Gateways to Spiritual Awakening*, Leonard Sweet decodes eleven genes that helped the United Methodist Church shift from a modern to a postmodern church. If a church fails to pass its DNA to the next generation, it could hasten biological extinction of the ecclesiastical species, because the next generation is not just any generation.[15]

The next generation of believers exists on an altered social landscape, the metaphorical moraine of postmodernism.[16] Millennial offspring represent a critical generational link of ecclesiastical DNA. One gene, the learning gene, holds the key that is necessary for the church's leadership today. "In one way, the learning gene shifts the church's focus from 'church growth' to 'church health,' says Sweet.[17]

This book will focus on an organic model that stresses church fitness so that leadership can engage a vision and mission that is relevant for the believing community.

Fitness Enthusiasm

Fitness implies continuation of the species including the ecclesiastical species of the church. Biologists have long been concerned about species survival because the alternative—extinction—is not good. One element that is needed to prevent the church's extinction is enthusiasm. The disciples, the apostle Paul, the Samaritan woman, Zacchaeus, and every person touched in one way or another by Jesus represent the new convert who becomes enthusiastic about his new life. Zacchaeus confessed his sin of cheating others and offered to repay them fourfold.[18] The lame man could not wait to tell anyone who would listen about his transformation.[19] The love of Jesus Christ has the power to make us a transformed witness about our relationship with him. The result of an unbeliever's transformation is to become enthusiastic about the One who transformed his life;

he wants to tell others about his defining moment. Are you enthusiastic about your relationship with Jesus Christ?

Sadly, this enthusiasm for evangelism often declines over time. Dr. John Hayward of the University of Glamorgan in the United Kingdom created an excellent mathematical model of church growth and decline, which helps to address the prevalence of declining church congregations and the extinction of many faith tribes.[20] Hayward believes that some Christians lose their enthusiasm for Christ over time. To partially explain the limitation of the enthusiastic period, Hayward says:

> The new believer not only loses their enthusiasm to recruit after a period of time, but also loses their network of unbelieving friends as they become integrated into the life of the church. It is possible for existing believers to have their enthusiasm rekindled, but not so easy for them to establish a network of potential converts.[21]

The role of the church is to combat this impulse to insularity by providing avenues to reach unbelievers with the love of Christ through ministry and mission opportunities. Matching spiritual gifts with appropriate ministry opportunities will keep the believing community fresh and excited. Too often believers are forced to work in roles that do not match their spiritual giftedness, leaving them frustrated, tired, and even burned out. Membership burnout accelerates when they are left doing work that should be done by church staff.

Having spiritual energy consumed by mundane church tasks without the making of disciples or witnessing to those in need can leave believers "rusted out."[22] After a time, members will feel used and unappreciated. The Holy Spirit is quenched in their lives. Leadership must provide a proper balance between work within the church and evangelism in order to augment the length of the any enthusiastic period.

If this enthusiasm dwindles and is never rekindled, it leaves a field of inactive members in its wake, causing a number of problems for the Kingdom. First, each member's relationship with Jesus may be compromised if the Holy Spirit is not fueled. Second, inactive members become poor witnesses to their community. Too many people say that "Christians are acting unChristian" and are therefore indistinguishable from unbelievers.[23] Third, inactive members place a burden on their churches. Their stewardship of time and labor is reduced. Their marginal cost increases, while their marginal benefit to the church diminishes.[24] Many inactive members become "free-riders" to their church by taking goods and services without giving back to the community.[25] Extending the enthusiastic period keeps a larger number of believers active in the church.

Dr. John Hayward's model underscores the importance of the church's ability to grow and sustain itself in believing communities.[26] Hayward demonstrates that a church needs to make enthusiasts, not just converts, if it is to avoid extinction. His model makes three assumptions:

1. "Unbelievers are converted, and recruited, into the church through contact with a subset of believers, called enthusiasts, or active believers.
2. After a period of time, the enthusiasts cease to be active in conversion, remaining in the church as inactive believers.
3. The enthusiastic period starts immediately after an unbeliever is converted."

In studying the major Christian sects in the UK, he found that a church's membership reaches equilibrium in its proportion of the population according to the potential of these enthusiasts to reproduce more enthusiasts. A church's reproduction potential (or rate of creating converts) is more important than excessive member losses in ensuring survival and preventing extinction. A church sees rapid revival growth when its reproduction potential is greater than its member losses.

Hayward's analysis shows that many Christian denominations in the UK are facing extinction because of high member losses coupled with a poor reproduction potential. In the U.S., where secularization is lower, these same church families suffer high member losses with borderline reproduction potential. On a hopeful note, he also demonstrates how a declining church can reverse its decline.

Churches can plot their membership number over time. Declining churches have a downward sloping line. The line is steeper in those churches with greater decline. The following figure shows Hayward's Recovery Curves.[27]

The slope of each line represents a church's aging curve. The dark solid line represents churches whose leaders have "no policy" or strategy to address the decline within their denomination or church. Without a strategy, survival is not sustainable and eventual extinction is inevitable. The point from which the remaining curves emerge, the inflection point, is the result of some intervention or change in policy on behalf of leadership within the ekklesia.

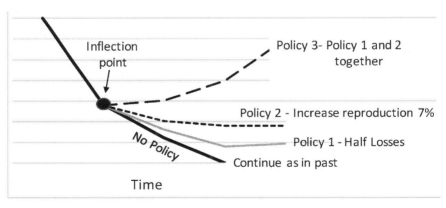

Hayward's Recovery Curves

Strategies to decrease member losses are represented by the light solid line. The policy puts strategies in place that keep members from leaving the church. Stemming losses alone delays extinction for a while and slows decline, but doesn't really change the culture or future of the church.

A more powerful result occurs when the church family improves its reproduction potential (illustrated by the dotted line). The trajectory changes slowly but eventually results in progressive growth. Halting the flow of people out of your doors helps, but not as much as converting new enthusiasts. *Faith Fitness* can provide the tools for understanding God's will for your church, making reproduction a natural by-product of fitness.

The dashed line demonstrates an ekklesia employing strategies that decrease losses while increasing reproduction through conversions. The end result is a dramatic level of growth. From the inflection point, an immediate explosion in revival growth occurs. Such genuine organic growth is the result of significant change in culture brought about by healthy people participating in best processes to yield God's product for each faith tribe.

Converting new enthusiasts and stemming losses requires a unique approach and commitment within the organization, one that few churches are able to replicate. The ability of a church to pass along its ecclesial genes is limited by its reproduction potential. If a church does not demonstrate fitness (the ability to grow new churches) in a growing population:

1. It is prone to the loss of active members, and merely stemming losses will not avert extinction.
2. A church may survive for a time, but it will lose its market share of people and secularization will close around her.[28]
3. Church vitality decreases as the percentage of inactive members increases.[29]

"Vitality" is the new buzzword for church health today. Vitality represents the presence of the Holy Spirit and the congregation's commitment to a church's vision and mission. Another name for vitality is member enthusiasm. The accompanying figure is a diagram of the Medcalfe-Sharp member enthusiasm model.[30] It shows the flux of members in and out of a church, and how members can increase or decrease their level of commitment. Enthusiasm is more than just active members. It represents a person who is indwelt by the Holy Spirit[31] and serves as a follower of Jesus Christ. One who has Jesus Christ, a new spirit, living in their heart, which has been transformed from a heart of stone into a heart of flesh.[32] This heart of flesh is ruled by the peace of Christ, and it clothes the body in virtues (compassion, kindness, humility, gentleness, and patience) that produce perfect unity within the church body through love.[33]

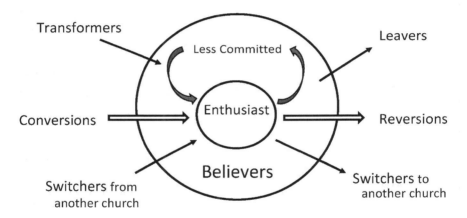

Member Enthusiasm Model

A church's pool of enthusiasts comes from different sources. New enthusiasts may come from outside the church as unbelievers who have converted, or they may be "switchers", enthusiasts who transfer from another church. Another source of enthusiasm comes from less-committed members who submit to the authority of Christ with a transformed heart and reaffirm their commitment to the church, "transformers". Their submission is expressed with renewed dedication through the giving of time (reflected in discipleship, shepherding, and ministry) and money and through their evangelism commitment. Any believing community lives with fluctuations in member activity ranging from individuals' conversions into the core set of committed believers to "leavers," who revert out of the enthusiastic core.

There are two groups of enthusiasts that are even more influential than transformers (believers who reaffirm their commitment to the church): newly converted enthusiasts, followed by the gathering of established enthusiasts in worship. Member enthusiasm is dropping in U.S. churches because of decreased conversions and increased numbers of uncommitted believers. Healthy church culture is suffering at the expense of waning member enthusiasm. An easy measure of member enthusiasm is to track the attendance of each member at worship services. If all members attended worship services, then the ratio of worship attendance to membership would be 1.0. If a church of 100 members attended worship along with, for example, ten visitors, then the ratio would be 100 + 10 or 1.1. If one half of the members attend worship, then the ratio is 0.5. This ratio is an easy marker for member enthusiasm because members are witnessing and bringing others to worship.[34]

Conservative sects maintain a fairly high worship attendance ratio over time, but mainline Protestant churches do not. Conservative Protestant sects tend to have a committed enthusiastic base. Members either attend with full activity or leave and join another congregation. Members are not allowed to simply stay on the membership rolls as an inactive or uncommitted member; therefore, worship attendance continues at a high percentage, especially because visitors are counted in the worship census. Conservative sects remove inactive members from their roles.

Mainline congregations experience fluctuating membership as one-time active members take on increasingly "inactive" roles. Most leavers do so quietly, and the churches they leave rarely get helpful exit information. Once discovered, pastors are reluctant to drop these leavers from their church roles, as it may reflect badly on their performance. Growing mainline churches have an attendance to member ratio of 0.56 or greater. Only 56 percent of their membership attends worship. Declining mainline churches have a ratio of 0.47, or about 47 percent member worship attendance. Dying churches fall to a ratio of less than 0.35, or 35 percent.

Congregations that are more organizationally complex, in that they have more committees and taskforces, are more affected by leavers (which creates a loss of labor). Congregations with more programming, ministries, and missions may be more susceptible to withholders, people who attend but don't tithe (which creates a loss of revenue). Both leavers and withholders significantly affect smaller congregations, whereas larger congregations enjoy economies of scale, which somewhat shields them from the effects of either.

Not all leavers are bad for a believing community. The fastest growing ekklesias with a strong vision and purpose also have the highest rate of leavers. These members leave because they don't agree with the community's godly vision, not because of any disagreement or conflict over a specific worship or leadership issue. A healthy church body will continue to grow even when people agree to disagree over the purpose of the Body in service to Christ. [35]

Not only are mainline denominations' worship-to-attendance ratios falling over time, but faltering churches within mainline denominations decrease even faster. This point of departure marks a significant change within the Body. The degree of conflict in a church is in direct proportion to its loss of vitality. By focusing on the stormy seas, we take our eyes off Jesus. We begin to sink. We lose hope.

The waxing and waning cycle of decline that embodies many churches over their lifespan is partly explained by Robert Dale. He wrote a book on how churches can revitalize by simply refocusing on Jesus, called *To Dream Again: How to Help Your Church Come Alive*.[36] Dale created "the health cycle model" of organizational behavior.

Robert Dale says that churches with a clarifying purpose create enthusiastic ministry. When churches accomplish their purpose, through maturing ministries, the ekklesia loses its focus. A believing community without a common vision of ministry only has the nostalgia of its glory days to celebrate; the members question each other, become polarized, and eventually drop out of the community.

The dilemma for leadership is to recognize when the Body is faltering so that proper emphasis is placed on vision and purpose again. He encourages leaders to reset their beliefs, goals, and structures. By creating a new common ministry, the church can come alive. Dale suggests that "planning links vision to implementation."[37] Churches without a purpose live in their past, tend to celebrate their birthdays, and enjoy homecoming services.

The key to a church ascending or sinking is a matter of direction. Any movement toward Jesus Christ is ascent.

Optimal Fitness

The last step in defining fitness is to look at the concept of "optimal" fitness. Fitness is optimal when a church is performing at its best despite limitations. I'm reminded about a person that I've never met, but who has always impressed me, Joni Erickson Tada. I heard her testimony on our local Christian radio station years ago, and I've listened to her speak about her ministries Joni and Friends and Wheels for the World.[38]

Joni has a heart to improve the daily lives of people with disabilities worldwide. She has created a loving community of support, prayer, and resources for people with disabilities. She herself became paralyzed after a diving accident when she was seventeen years old (over fifty years ago). Her body has extreme limitations, but she has accepted her condition as one that she cannot change during her time on earth. She has learned to serve the Lord in an optimal way. Despite her physical limitations, Joni Erickson Tada has been in service to the Lord through Joni and Friends, her ministry for disabled people.

Optimal fitness means not only that a church understands and accepts its own limitations, but also that it performs optimally in the Kingdom despite limitations that make service to the Lord difficult. As we discussed, the churches of Smyrna[39] and Philadelphia[40] are two great examples of an ekklesia living in optimal fitness because they served the Lord despite geographic and political obstacles. Optimal fitness gives every church a chance; none are excluded, none have excuses. Optimal fitness allows every church onto the field to run the race of life. Optimal fitness creates a lifestyle with a new expectation of wellness, one that will not be limited by previous generations' mistakes.

The health of a church is established as a subjective assessment by the leadership, by the believing community (Body), or by a church care consultant. It should be based upon the building of community with the presence of the Holy Spirit and upon being perfected in the love of Christ. Wellness includes the personal responsibility of the believing community in contributing to their own health. I will use the term "wellness" to include an emphasis on managing disease and prolonging life for service. As we have seen earlier in this chapter, a disease is any abnormal condition that prevents the body from operating effectively. Examples include sin, conflict, and clergy or leader dysfunction.

Fitness involves wellness of the believing community for the expressed purpose of building up the next generation of fit followers and of planting the heart of Christ in the hearts of their neighbors. This is not limited by, but includes new church starts. Optimal fitness speaks to the corporate participation in the spiritual race despite the internal or external limitations that an ekklesia may not be able to change. Every church has enthusiasts. With the appropriate fitness lifestyle, these enthusiasts can help transform their ekklesia to live with purpose within the Kingdom.

The comparison between a fit church culture and Body and the fit human body is useful. This fitness concept helps church leaders understand the collective condition of their membership. Creating an organization that pursues the ingredients necessary to sustain a healthy ekklesia will reestablish God's holiness, improve member enthusiasm, and build fit followers for the Kingdom.

	Church	Human body
Health	Functionality without self, sin, & stressors	Functionality without disease, infection, or environmental stressors
Wellness	Leadership establishing proper training habits to render good spiritual health	Good mental and physical health due to deliberate diet, exercise, work, and habits
Fitness	Adapting to the environment to build up and to plant the gospel into the next generation of followers	Adapting to the environment to transmit the genotype into the next generation
Optimal Fitness	Fitness despite limitations	Fitness despite limitations
Enthusiast	Believer who is a full participant in the vision and mission of the believing community	Passionate about fitness

Fitness Corollary

Disease

The popular AMC TV series *The Walking Dead*, with its opening disclaimer, has intrigued me.[41] Supposedly a mutated virus has infected people worldwide, creating lifeless shells of people—zombies—,who purposelessly walk around and feed on others. To make matters worse, these "undead" people seem to be capable of functioning on just one small part of their infected brain; therefore, they're hard to eliminate. Living people also have a low level of the virus, but it doesn't get activated until a zombie bites them or they die another way. Joining the lifeless community of the dead seems like an inevitability to the living. Nonetheless, the declining ranks of living people try to avoid becoming a food source for the zombies, forming small, secure colonies of survivors in hopes of finding a cure. Ironically, because of likely extinction, the survivors are the ones known as "the walking dead."

Sounds like a classic zombie movie plot, right? Only now the graphics are more explicit and the story becomes more compelling as the writers and producers emotionally draw viewers into the personal reality of characters attempting to survive. Could it be that the original version of this plot was evident in the Bible and commented on by Jesus many years ago? There is a parallel between this storyline and the one in Jesus's condemnation of the church in Ephesus: "I know your deeds; you have a reputation of being alive, but you are dead."[42] Like zombies, the Ephesus Christians were busy in life and seeking to only satisfy themselves. Are increasing populations of dead churchgoers taking over U.S. churches at the expense of a living minority who seek to be relevant?

The hymns of the early Christians often referred to sinners who were separated from God as being asleep or even dead. In Ephesians 5:14, Paul says, "Wake up, sleeper, rise from the dead, and Christ will shine on you." So many churches have believers who only go through the motions of a spiritual life, but in fact are unable to demonstrate evidence of the living Christ in their hearts. In many churches, dead Christians outnumber committed, enthusiastic believers. Instead of a mutated virus, original sin inhabits man and threatens to take over the body of Christ when members become dead to their purpose in Christ. Churchgoers become desensitized by living with sin and disease. This exposure may lead to complacency and selfishness.

The spiritual life and culture of these churches are compromised. When a church loses its enthusiastic core of believers to less committed Christians, the faith, works, and Mind of Christ are also lost. The fit church culture slowly evaporates and becomes a less healthy version of itself. This degradation of church culture can be slow and insidious. I pray that the brave among us will have our eyes open to the afflictions of his dying churches and that the Holy Spirit will help leaders create a free and fearless response to bring health and vitality back to our communities.

We have studied what Jesus said in Scripture about the dysfunctional churches in the book of Revelation. Now let's look at how disease can limit churches and diminish a fit organizational culture. Disease is an abnormal condition affecting the body or part of the body, especially as a consequence of infection, inherent weakness, or environmental stress that impairs normal physiological functioning.[43] This definition of disease is suitable for the human condition as well as the spiritual condition of a believing community. This definition can be rewritten as an abnormal condition affecting the Body (believing community), especially as a consequence of sin, self, or stressors that impair normal Christ-centered functioning. But don't despair! While these conditions are serious, they are not irreversible or terminal.

Infection, then, is one affliction within a church. Infection begins as small and insidious and incubates for a time before it overwhelms the body, impairing optimal function. Infection is usually superficial and limited to one tissue or body space. But if it's allowed to fester untreated, infection can spread to other areas, becoming systemic. It prevents fitness by limiting vitality, energy, and even the power to survive.

In the Church, sin can take the form of any number of infections, which afflict the body of Christ. Sin imposes its carnal nature on the body, making the body a slave to the infection.[44] Sin can be personal or corporate. Individual sin in leaders may lead to corporate sin within the church. In Romans 7:19-20 the apostle Paul says, "For I do not do the good I want to do, but the evil I do not want to do—this I keep on doing. Now if I do what I do not want to do, it is no longer I who do it, but it is sin living in me that does it."

It is a fact that every church intermittently gets superficial infections. The complex nature of the institution sometimes prevents early recognition. Few churches proactively treat the infections that wage war against the members of her Body, leaving her weak, weary, and wanting. Any number of infections could be responsible. A wellness-oriented church is quick to respond to conflicts, poor personnel management, or financial stressors, thereby preventing long-lasting repercussions.

Most parenting experts agree that proper love, nurturing, and training help children develop properly. The same is true for the Body of Christ. Both ordained and non-ordained leaders are necessary to build the church and plant the Word of God. Pope Francis has been reforming the administrative structures of the Catholic church, and he recognizes the liability of unhealthy leaders. He recently discussed the diseases of leadership. Church leaders should be more experienced and spiritually mature; however, he writes:

> Leaders are susceptible to an array of debilitating maladies, including arrogance, intolerance, myopia and pettiness. When those diseases go untreated, the organization itself is enfeebled. To have a healthy church, we need healthy leaders. Leaders should be held to a higher standard, since their scope of influence makes their ailments particularly infectious.[45]

Patricia St. John, author and dedicated missionary to Morocco, deconstructs the Old Testament book of Numbers to discuss the sins of God's people and their leaders. She describes how the nation of Israel missed out on God's blessings. His people indulged in small, "respectable" sins. The sins of the people included complaining, unbelief, and pride. Their leaders had a surfeit of jealousy, pride, spiritual depression, and impatience. The result was that "They could not enter in." [to Canaan][46] Are we in God's churches missing the Way because we have chosen a lesser path? A wellness-oriented church manages these corporate sins so its people can enjoy the more excellent path prepared by the Holy Spirit.

The second category for disease is an inherent weakness within the Body itself. The weakness can be genetic, physical, or developmental. A genetic weakness includes denominational affiliation or doctrinal allegiance. A member may like his church but not agree with some of the denominational tenets. Some members are drawn to a church because of its doctrinal biases. Sometimes doctrinal allegiance is a stronger driver of commitment than allegiance to Christ.

An important specialty in medicine is allergy and immunology. The human body has a remarkable ability to make antibodies when exposed to allergens (either in the air or in foods). Even infections or trauma can trigger these immune responses; however, in their vigor to rid the body of these irritants and infections, sometimes the antibodies end up attacking healthy tissue. Such diseases include those of the bones and joints (arthritis), brain and spine (lupus and neuritis), intestines (Crohn's disease), muscles (polymyositis), and skin (many dermatitises), etc. Therefore, the autoimmune system can sometimes actually harm the very body it is designed to protect.

In the Body of Christ, false doctrines, idolatry, and false teaching can be introduced, causing inflammation that leads to conflict as the Body attacks and destroys itself. The Body is then left weak and susceptible to invasion by other forces (sin) and principalities (Satan). The Body has a natural propensity to heal itself, but with an inherent weakness, the Body can lose its gospel programming, Christ-centeredness, and natural functioning.

Physical limitations include membership size, structure, and limited resources. Churches cannot change their location unless they grow and expand. Rural churches have challenges just like urban churches. Resources are tied to assets and revenue. Living a fitness lifestyle is the only remedy for this inherent weakness.

Examples of developmental weakness are leadership, education, and training. Leaders are selected in many ways and for many different reasons, but not all leaders are prepared spiritually for the task. Leadership development is important for both ordained and non-ordained leaders. One of the most important inherent weaknesses within a faltering ekklesia is dysfunctional ordained and/or non-ordained leadership. Leaders who are weak in faith make poor decisions for the ekklesia. The Psalmist Asaph chronicles the life of Israel's unfaithful nation and the consequences of their unbelief: "Therefore their days He consumed in futility, and their years in fear."[47] Self and Christ are inversely proportional; the self increases at the expense of Christ.

Ordained leaders can become an inherent weakness through lack of spiritual authority, overwork, or spiritual exhaustion. The vocation of ordination should be a call to the power or *exousia* of Christ, not to the pastor or priest's power. God awards the spiritual authority for a task through his call. The lack of authentic spiritual authority among clergy is a major contributor to stunted and starved churches becoming barren with a hard heart. The life of ordained leaders is not easy though. It depends on discipline, prayer, faith, and trust.

Clergy work long, difficult schedules; they tend to have workweeks of fifty or more hours and have more unpredictable schedules than those in many other professions. Over time, long work hours can contribute to exhaustion and burnout. Keeping that in mind, a Duke Divinity study showed that clergy have an obesity rate of 39.7 percent for pastors thirty-four to sixty-four years old, which is ten percent higher than the general population. For clergy in the age range of forty-five to fifty-four years, the rate is 14.2 percent higher. Consequently, clergy have a higher rate of health problems including diabetes, arthritis, hypertension, asthma, and poor eating habits.[48]

Every church should provide a gym membership for its clergy. In addition, time from every day should be devoted to exercise. Clergy should maintain continuing education and be allowed to travel with other clergy for support and encouragement. Clergy complacency or spiritual boredom can lead to a calculated apathy, an inherent weakness that the church cannot afford to have.

God sees our clergy's weaknesses and asks, "What are you doing here?"[49] Many of our clergy have lost their educative will, their ability to wait on God, and their contemplative powers. They can use the complex organizational church structure as a shield to hide financial insecurity, faithlessness, spiritual boredom, or a lack of enthusiasm. The loss of motivation to lead fellow believers into the future by the promise of God's hope leads to a crisis within a church's heart.

Clergy can reclaim their vitality and enthusiasm for their call to ministry by participating in effectual continuing education, interacting with other clergy, and spending time on improving their own personal health.[50] But if ordained leadership doesn't take personal responsibility for their own wellness, should we be surprised that their church lacks a wellness orientation?

One of the most important roles of leaders is to manage conflict. It takes healthy, faithful leaders to prevent a community from serving themselves instead of Jesus Christ.[51] "What causes fights and quarrels among you?" James asks this question of believers in the early church and then proceeds to answer his own question with another question: "Don't they come from your desires that battle within you?"[52] He points to wrong motives, seeking personal pleasure, and siding with the world in affairs relating to God and his church. He calls these fighters and quarrelers in the church "adulterous people," spiritually unfaithful to "the spirit he caused to live in us."[53] God longs for our faithfulness and love, and his Holy Spirit is jealous for our full devotion. Conflict arises because of the presence of the world in man separating him spiritually from the purpose and vision of God's Church. Paul talks about the effect of conflict in the Corinthian church as causing "divisions among you." Instead, Paul urges them, "brothers and sisters, in the name of our Lord Jesus Christ, that all of you agree with one another in what you say and that there be no divisions among you, but that you be perfectly united in mind and thought."[54]

David A. Roozen's work out of the Hartford Institute for Religion Research, published as a result of the Faith Communities Today (FACT) national surveys of American congregations, is one of the best sources of information about congregational life. His comprehensive FACT survey is called "American Congregations."[55] He shows that 75 percent of congregations have had a conflict in the past five years (of the time period the study examined) in one of four key areas: worship, finances, programs, or leadership priorities.

Worship style is a cause of both congregational growth and conflict. This kind of internal tension is common, but avoidable. "True worshippers shall worship the Father in spirit and in truth: for the Father seeketh such to worship him. God is a Spirit: and they that worship him must worship in spirit and in truth."[56] Worship is always the result of the presence of God. It is not something that can be forced. Too often we have worship leaders trying to replace the Holy Spirit. The best preparation for worship is not rehearsal, but surrender. Anyone participating in worship should be wholly submitted to the work of the Holy Spirit. Worship is something God bestows based upon the inward disposition of our hearts toward God. It is both spiritual and emotional: a feeling in the heart that is appropriately expressed. The apostle Paul told the Roman believers that the only true way to worship God was to yield up their bodies to him as "living sacrifices."[57] To truly worship God is to fully surrender ourselves to him. Churches must allow different styles of worship to coexist in a productive and supportive setting.

Church research clearly demonstrates that offering multiple kinds of worship services is associated with church vitality and growth.[58,59] When believers have a choice of worship settings, they are more likely to experience the presence of God during such worship. True worship has little to do with liturgical style, orientation, or location; it has more to do with the sincerity of one's heart to the heavenly Father. Church leaders must understand the importance of worship to the praise and intimacy of God, the place of worship to the corporate unity of the ekklesia, and the power of worship to draw the presence of the Holy Spirit to the children of God.

Another potential source of conflict is financial tension. For too many churches, the finance committee wields too much power, the power of the purse. Except for megachurches, most churches' balance sheets are actually fairly simple. Congregational giving is the main source of revenue, and in most churches the annual budget is set based upon that stream of income. Programs and ministries can become casualties of the budget, especially during this age of congregational decline.

Conflict arises over staff salaries, cost of living increases, and the percent of the budget dedicated to missions. A typical cycle includes clashes of leadership over budget constraints, morale problems of the staff over financial concerns, and increasing focus on the finances, which causes alarm among the Body. Worsening finances contribute to conflict and erode spiritual vitality. In most cases, poor leadership choices cause members to lose enthusiasm and decrease their contributions, which stimulates conflict. The result is that the mission of the church is not fulfilled. Healthy finances, on the other hand, do not relate to either the presence of spiritual vitality or a conflict-free congregation. Without sanctifying prayer and active faith, a robust church budget only promotes spiritual mediocrity and halfway discipleship. The positive relationship between spiritual vitality and financial health holds regardless of congregational health.[60]

Conflict causes many congregants to lose confidence in their leadership. After all, shouldn't ordained clergy and lay leaders be able to solve these problems? Members of different religious organizations handle conflict uniquely. The preferred Evangelical response to conflict is mobility; "leavers" vote with their feet. The Catholic and Orthodox approach is to rotate leadership. "Withholders" are older, mainline Protestant members who tend to withhold resources like money to voice their displeasure with conflict. In Roozen's study, although 67 percent of congregations had only one conflict, one third of congregations had two or more sources of conflict in the previous five years.[61]

The last category causing disease in the Body is environmental stress. Any circumstance that consumes the Body's energy for self-preservation instead of expressing the love of Christ in ministry and mission can be a stressor. Usually these are external forces, which cause dysfunction within the Body. The Body of Christ retrenches where famine, war-ravaged corridors, or religious or political oppression or conflict exists. At present, these are mainly international churches; however, opposition to Christians and churches in the U.S. is increasing. In addition, conflict over social issues can be a source of environmental stress on a church.

The insidious injection of the unbelieving world into the Body's DNA prevents the Word and works of the Lord from being reproduced by the next generation of believers. Its toxins poison the Christian heritage among the servants of tomorrow. Believers struggle with living in the world without being of the world. The world encourages a life of easy pleasures. Ekklesias, which haven't reconciled the tension between the world and real spiritual life, can develop a type of soul-sickness, a dysfunctional, artificial, self-induced life.

A thin line exists between stressors that render a Body dysfunctional versus those that serve as tests to prove and refine the Body's faith.[62] Leadership and the adaptive skills needed to handle these stressors are either nonexistent or inadequate in faltering churches. Ideally, these stressors serve as trials of adversity, tragedy, or suffering, which build unity, maturity, service, and leadership within the Body. However, some churches are simply too dysfunctional to develop the fruit of the Spirit when trials or opportunities present themselves.

> The Church will outlive the universe;
> in it the individual person will outlive the universe.
> C.S. Lewis[63]

Fitness Moment

- There are important organizational distinctions between health, wellness, fitness, and optimal fitness.
- Wellness is the organization's attempt to maintain focus on Christ, limit dysfunction, and prevent disease.
- Fitness is adapting to the environment to build up and plant the gospel in the next generation of followers.
- Optimal fitness is the fullest expression of a healthy church culture.
- Enthusiasm is the contagion that drives an ekklesia.

- Disease is a natural part of the human body and a church organization, but it must be managed.
- Repentance is a necessary step to turn away from sin and to develop a healthy culture and fit church.

Repent

Sig: *follow the instructions*
Refill(s): *prn — as needed*
Comments: *No substitutions permitted*

I will give you a new heart and put a new spirit in you;
I will remove from you your heart of stone
and give you a heart of flesh.
Ezekiel 36:26

You have read about fit New Testament ekklesias as well as unhealthy New Testament churches. At this point can you objectively discern the spiritual condition of your ekklesia? Sometimes it's hard to perform a personal assessment. Discouragement, bias, pride, defiance, skepticism, and sinfulness may prevent honesty.

After the Jews returned to Jerusalem from their captivity in Babylon, they became religiously cold and morally lax and forgot to love God and their fellow citizens too. The Jews were more than backsliders. The priests became irreverent and neglectful.[64] Being careless, marrying idol worshipers,[65] robbing God of his tithes and offerings,[66] and the growing prevalence of social sin[67] were all sins that slowly turned them from God. Habakkuk told the Jews to live by faith.

Zechariah prophesied for them to turn to God, and Malachi urged them to repent and return to God.[68]

Repentance is a prominent doctrine in Scripture. The Hebrew Bible discusses repentance in the Old Testament. The word "repent" is used thirty-four times in the King James Version. In the New Testament, "repent" is commanded by Jesus and Peter,[69] John the Baptist,[70] and Paul.[71] In John's vision in Revelation, Jesus chastises the people of five churches for their sin and selfishness. Jesus calls his wandering children from these churches to repent.

Repentance is usually thought of as a complex personal action; however, in addition to the five churches mentioned in Revelation, it is a command used for *groups* of people: men at Nineveh,[72] crowds of young enthusiasts in Judea,[73] and "those in Damascus, then to those in Jerusalem and in all Judea, and then to the Gentiles."[74] Today, commanding a body of believers to repent also seems appropriate because sin can be a corporate act. The problem is for that body to recognize its sin.

The dictionary defines "repenting" as turning from sin and dedicating oneself to the amendment of one's life.[75] The Latin root for repent, *repoenitere*, means to feel regret. The New Testament Greek Lexicon suggests the origin to be *metanoeo*, to change one's mind.[76] "Repentance is primarily a change of moral purpose, a sudden and often violent reversal of the soul's direction."[77] Repentance is a radical change in one's life as a whole. The act of repentance requires emotion to feel regret and both intellect and will to change one's mind. "Repent, then, and turn to God, so that your sins may be wiped out, that times of refreshing may come from the Lord."[78]

On the cross, Jesus said, "Father, forgive them, for they do not know what they are doing."[79] His forgiveness leads to a repentant heart. Do we want to be healed? He died that we could have life, abundant life. He is ready to receive us. We must identify our sins and confess them at the cross. Do we want to be holy and whole again? Do we want our churches to be holy and whole again? We must repent of our sins. We can listen and hear him say, "If my people, who are called by my name, will humble themselves and pray and seek my face and turn from their wicked ways, then I will hear from heaven and forgive their sin and heal their land."[80]

Unfortunately, too many church leaders haven't come to their senses. Like the prodigal son, a diet of pods from the pigs' pen leads only to malnutrition and faltering health. But a nutritious banquet awaits those who choose to return to their Father for warmth, significance, and health.[81] Without repentance, *Faith Fitness* and this prescription cannot restore the fortunes of your ekklesia.

To confess, to be forgiven, and to repent will mean a different lifestyle. To be healed will mean a different responsibility. To be whole will mean a different functionality in the Kingdom. God will remove the stony heart from our body and replace it with a healthy heart,[82] but the key to a changed heart is repentance. Any church body can choose to repent of spiritual shortcomings due to a dysfunctional heart. The Revelation churches that Jesus condemned were given a stern warning to repent. The response to our shortcomings should be the same. The choice is ours, but if we fail to repent, then God will do with us as he wills. This choice represents the right response and also activates a cascade of spiritual blessings. One of God's greatest blessings is that he forgives our trespasses and remembers our sins no more.[83]

Upon reading the chapter "Church Culture," it should become clear that every church has to constantly manage their own wellness. Part of that process is recognizing our corporate spiritual depravity and repenting of our selfishness and spiritual shortcomings. Some churches automatically do this as part of their communion ritual. Be careful, because the ritual must be sincere. A changed heart only comes to those who turn away from their sins and toward God. Leadership can be so consumed with the administrative details of organizational life that wellness cannot be obtained, because the important step of repentance is omitted.

4

FITNESS TOOLBOX

By the grace God has given me,
I laid a foundation as a wise builder.
Paul

W̲e have already learned about the diseases that limit church health and examined the fit church archetype and the ingredients of a healthy church. How does a modern-day church become fit for service? Let's focus on the tools that help leaders to ascend the fitness spectrum to create a fit church.

Many models have been attempted, but few stand out as instructive to leaders or are relevant for today's religious context. A functionally relevant model is a church body that has the mind and heart of Christ and that does the will of Christ. The model begins with a sure footing and with Jesus Christ as the cornerstone and foundation.

The Bible, the inspired Word of God, supplies the actual building blocks for this fit church model. Scripture offers context into the proper function of believing communities, and biblical metaphors give affirmation to the healthy church archetype that has been discussed. The building blocks are connected by mortar, the human element. Typically, mortar is water and sand; in this case, it represents two man-made ingredients that can strengthen churches. The first is the sage advice of modern-day apostles, the ordained theologians who have lived, studied, and written on this subject from a biblical perspective. Many of these pastors and former pastors have lived in the trenches where the rubber of believers' souls meets the road of church life.

The second comes from academic researchers, whose carefully crafted studies link important variables that make up a healthy church. These scholars share both academic theories and scientific insights into determinants of church health.

The insights from people who approach the ekklesia from a biblical perspective and from others who study religious organizations from an academic perspective can combine to form a relevant mortar for the American church construct. These man-made contributors form a unique type of bond, which allows the building blocks to rise upon the foundation in the construction of a fit church.

Biblical Tools

Jesus

The most important church driver of spiritual fitness is Jesus Christ himself. In several Scriptures (Ephesians 2:20, 1 Peter 2:6, and Isaiah 28:16), the noun *akrogôniaios* is used to symbolically link Jesus to a foundational stone, the first stone upon which the remainder of the building is built. A cornerstone is the point of intersection where at least two walls meet. In the New Testament, Jesus was the living cornerstone where the walls of the Jews and of the Gentiles met to become his Church. The Church includes many members who make up the body of Christ.[1] The body is unified "so that there should be no division in the body, but that its parts should have equal concern for each other."[2]

In building a fit church, the truth of Christ in Scripture intersects with the wisdom of man (mostly ordained leaders as well as non-ordained leaders and followers). The concept of man's Christology is therefore important. Jesus was a man glorified, raised from the dead to a position of lordship at the right hand of God. Jesus Christ is the head of the Church,[3] "one God and Father of all, who is over all and through all and in all."[4] "He was God with men," and, "He is Man with God. But more than this, He is heir of all things, Lord of all worlds, Head of the Church and the Firstborn of the new creation. He is the way to God, the life of the believer, the hope of Israel and the high priest of every true worshiper. He holds the keys to death and hell and stands as advocate and surety for everyone who believes on Him in truth."[5]

Placing Jesus at the headship of our churches is an important starting point on the journey toward church fitness. "And God placed all things under his feet and appointed him to be head over everything for the church, which is his body, the fullness of him who fills everything in every way."[6] A healthy ekklesia has leaders who live out this truth in all the decisions of the church. Every leader within the church body should be under the direction of the Head. Leaders, especially ordained leaders, can recapture the power of early churches by using the Mind of Christ to direct decisions that become the heart and soul of their ekklesia.

Bible and Bible Metaphors

The Word of God contains the wisdom to understand spiritual fitness, and Scripture should provide the basic building blocks for any fit church. Scripture reveals the true heart of Jesus in his Church. Jesus is not only the Head of the Church, but as the Holy Spirit, he should also be the heartbeat of every church. In the fit assembly, the epicenter of church decision-making is from the Way, the Truth, and the Life. How seriously do church leaders depend upon his Word?

A church organization must emulate the culture and essence of its ultimate leader by replicating his vision, purpose, focus, and mission. Too often, we choose our way. Our conduct leaves little doubt that we are not much influenced by his teaching. God must have his way if churches are to be fit. In Acts 8:21, Peter told Simon, "You have no part or share in this ministry, because your heart is not right before God." A church's heart is right when it represents the heart of Christ.

The Bible uses over ninety metaphors for the church. Jesus, in his teachings, used colorful metaphors to give insight to the disciples and to those who had "ears to hear." Biblical metaphors highlight the best practices among his most fit churches. The biblical metaphors of the Bride, the Branch, and the Body are deeply insightful for churches. These metaphors help explain the function of a fit church today by clarifying the biblical ingredients displayed by the Thessalonian, Philadelphian, and Smyrnan New Testament churches, and by displaying the Mind of Christ.

The Bride

Say Yes to the Dress, *Bridezilla*, and *Bride Wars* are all "reality" TV shows taking advantage of the raw emotions associated with the wedding process. Angry words, conflicts, self-indulgence, and destroyed relationships are the rule on these shows. Sometimes people demonstrating the most raucous behavior are rewarded with the most attention, even if they do not get their own way. This sounds too much like some of our churches at times. Too many families (and church families) have survived the chaos, only to leave much debris on the battlefield of good intentions.

The unique period of time between the engagement and the wedding is what I call the "wedding wait." All attention turns to the enormous preparation for the wedding, that climatic moment when all eyes are on the beautiful, prepared bride. This turns out to be a metaphor for the Church, who is also waiting: waiting for the return of the bridegroom, Jesus.

When my daughters married, I was so impressed with their attitudes and witness during their own "wedding waits." They kept the focus off of themselves and primarily on their new bridegrooms. Their purpose was to prepare themselves for the lives they would have together. Each daughter was the consummate bride-in-waiting.

What do weddings have to do with a fit church? Altogether, these wedding metaphors paint a picture of the unique relationship between Christ and his Church. John the Baptist testified to his own disciples that Jesus was like the bridegroom (the most important man at the wedding) and that he, John, was like the "friend" or best man. The Scripture in the Gospel of John exclaims, "The bride belongs to the bridegroom."[7] Paul continued the image of Jesus as the bridegroom and the Church as the bride when he promised the Corinthian believers to "one husband," Jesus Christ.[8] In the same comparison, he also described Christ as the head of the church.[9] In Matthew 25:1-13, Jesus educated his disciples about the Kingdom of heaven, and he compared the church to the bride(s)-in-waiting for the bridegroom to arrive at the wedding banquet. This so called "wedding wait" sets an instructive tone for the church's vision and direction in this earthly kingdom. The bride contributes to the fit church by exhibiting the proper attitude, character, and tone of her second-coming attitude to her bridegroom, Jesus Christ, her *raison d'être*.

During my daughters' wedding-waits, they prepared daily with diligence and single-minded focus on their vision of togetherness with their grooms. On one level, that diligence played out in staying physically fit (so that they could look their best in their wedding dresses). They also maintained their spiritual well-being by meeting with their pastor regularly, reading Scripture daily, and devoting time for regular prayer. Each bride had a circle of friends that could encourage her and keep her accountable during the process. Basically, they kept balance in their lives, but it took a great deal of discipline and work.

The vision for churches today is to run the race for and to keep their eyes on the prize: Jesus. A church should seek to transform itself through the perfecting work of the Holy Spirit so that she will be a sufficient bride for a bridegroom of whom God says, "This is my Son, whom I love; with him I am well pleased."[10] The bride metaphor speaks to the discipline required for us to work out our salvation so that God can work in us. The bride metaphor also demonstrates the intelligent choice of bringing the best part of ourselves into life-giving fellowship with God so that we can enjoy the "Shalom," or the harmonious, caring community with God at its center.

The wedding-wait, then, becomes a period of anticipation in reaching for a vision that is worthwhile and is, as Henri Nouwen says, "our only necessary thing!" As the bride of Christ, every church should have a second-coming attitude, a single-minded focus, and a suffering devotion to Jesus, the bridegroom.

The Branch

Just as a man and woman become one in marriage, Paul says, "But he who unites himself with the Lord is one with him in spirit."[11] Another biblical metaphor to demonstrate a church's oneness with Christ is the "Vine and Gardener" passage described by Jesus in John 15:1-2 and 4-13:

> I am the true vine, and my Father is the gardener. He cuts off every branch in me that bears no fruit, while every branch that does bear fruit he prunes so that it will be even more fruitful. Remain in me, as I also remain in you. No branch can bear fruit by itself; it must remain in the vine. Neither can you bear fruit unless you remain in me. I am the vine; you are the branches. If you remain in me and I in you, you will bear much fruit; apart from me you can do nothing. If you do not remain in me, you are like a branch that is thrown away and withers; such branches are picked up, thrown into the fire and burned. If you remain in me and my words remain in you, ask whatever you wish, and it will be done for you. This is to my Father's glory, that you bear much fruit, showing yourselves to be my disciples. As the Father has loved me, so have I loved

you. Now remain in my love. If you keep my commands, you will remain in my love, just as I have kept my Father's commands and remain in his love. I have told you this so that my joy may be complete. My command is this: love each other as I have loved you. Greater love has no one than this: to lay down one's life for one's friends.

To produce the fruit that the gardener (God) desires, we the branches must remain attached to the source of our sustenance: the mercy and love flowing through the vine (Jesus). The primary focus of every believing community is to remain connected to Jesus. The passion of every believing community should be to bear much fruit, a fruit that is unique to each church's own special character and strengths. But first we must surrender in Christ and be intimately connected to him at all times so that his love and fragrance are represented in the fruit we bear.

A fit church must also be steadfast in the Word. The act of gripping the hands of Jesus should be as firm as the graft on a plant. We should have an intimate closeness with the compass in our life.

After my father retired, he busied himself with many hobbies. One involved grafting together different species of plants. One day I was admiring his work and looking over the plants. I noticed that some of the newer grafts were tied with a band. The older ones had grown together, making a tight bond that ultimately was stronger than any other part of the branch. The branches need time to form this natural bond to their new source of energy and life. Fit churches are similar. Staying connected to the Word is essential for growth. Only by constant contact with the vine over time can our bond with God be strong and lasting.

Another insight from the branch metaphor is that the fit church must produce fruit. The gardener, God, requires fruit from our branches. Our fruit contains the sweetness of God's love, and can look, feel, smell, and taste unique to our own individuality and gifts. Every fruit contains seeds with the potential to grow new trees, fruit-bearing trees. The truth is that this is why we're here: to produce fruit. John the Baptist warned the crowds to, "Produce fruit in keeping with repentance," and that, "every tree that does not produce good fruit will be cut down and thrown into the fire."[12] Jesus gives examples of this fruit as sharing our food and clothes with the needy and treating people fairly.

After Jesus cleared the temple and was leaving for Bethany, he saw a fig tree in full leaf. The trees around Jerusalem bore fruit once they reached a full canopy of leaves. When Jesus approached the tree and found no fruit, he cursed the tree, "May no one ever eat fruit from you again." The next morning the tree was withered from the roots.[13] What good is a fig tree without fruit? Many of our churches have beautiful leaves but bear no fruit. Could this be why so many churches are slowly dying?

The gardeners maximized production by pruning the branches; this creates healthy growth for abundant produce. A bushy tree with a full canopy of many healthy branches can produce more fruit than one large self-serving branch whose only purpose is to produce just enough leaves to help maintain it; fruit would only take energy and attention away from such a branch.

In *Spirituality for Ministry*, Urban T. Holmes describes the process well:[14]

Any good gardener knows that beautiful roses require careful pruning. Pieces of living plants have to die. It cannot just grow wild. We cannot simply "celebrate growth." It is more than to be regretted, it is tragic that we seem to have lost the insight that growth in Christ requires careful pruning. Pieces of us by our intentional action need to die if we are to become the person that is in God's vision. We are not cutting away a cancerous growth, but making room for intended growth. Mortification refers to that intentional action of pruning of life that better life might grow by God's grace—just as better roses grow by God's grace.

While the gardener carefully prunes, our part is to do some self-pruning also. For both the Church and the individual believer, the practice of removing that part of us that is not wholly surrendered to God is healthy maintenance. Evelyn Underhill in *The Spiritual Life* says it best:[15]

> Mortification means dealing with ourselves; mortification means killing the very roots of self-love; pride and possessiveness, anger and violence, ambition and greed in all their disguises, however respectable those disguises may be, whatever uniforms they wear... Indeed, wherever we find people whose spiritual life is robust and creative, we find that in one way or another this transformation has been affected and this price has been paid.

The branch metaphor reveals a two-fold truth about a fit church: our focus is to remain in Jesus by attending to God, and our passion is to produce much fruit by dealing with ourselves—pruning ourselves out of the way so that we can be in harmony with God's vision. The branches, just like churches and individuals, enthusiastically grow to fulfill their purpose. The branch metaphor tells "why" the Church runs the race. A church as the branch gives focus and passion to its ekklesia.

The Body

Paul used the metaphor of the church as a body in three main passages. In Colossians, Paul addressed the Colossian heresy by exalting Christ as the head of the body, the church.[16] He told the Colossians that the whole body had lost connection with the head, who supports, sustains, and grows the body.[17]

The imagery of the body growing under the direction of the head, Christ, continues in Ephesians 4:1-16. The central theme of this metaphor is to grow in maturity with Christ and to grow in unity among believers. This growing process results in a believing community perfecting their work of ministry by carrying out the mission of the church together.

Finally, the church as body of Christ metaphor in 1 Corinthians 12:12-27 completes our understanding of the mission of the Church. First, let's read the Scripture:

> Just as a body, though one, has many parts, but all its many parts form one body, so it is with Christ. For we were all baptized by one Spirit so as to form one body—whether Jews or Gentiles, slave or free—and we were all given the one Spirit to drink. Even so the body is not made up of one part but of many. Now if the foot should say, "Because I am not a hand, I do not belong to the body," it would not for that reason stop being part of the body. And if the ear should say, "Because I am not an eye, I do not belong to the body," it would not for that reason stop being part of the body. If the whole body were an eye, where would the sense of hearing be? If the whole body were an ear, where would the sense of smell be? But in fact God has placed the parts in the body, every one of them, just as he wanted them to be. If they were all one part, where would the body be? As it is, there are many parts, but one body. The eye cannot say to the hand, "I don't need you!" And the head cannot say to the feet, "I don't need you!" On the contrary, those parts of the body that seem to be weaker are indispensable, and the parts that we think are less honorable we treat with special honor. And the parts that are unpresentable are treated with special modesty, while our presentable parts need no special treatment. But God has put the body together, giving greater honor to the parts that lacked it, so that there should be no division in the body, but that its parts should have equal concern for each other. If one part suffers, every part suffers with it; if one part is honored, every part rejoices with it. Now you are the body of Christ, and each one of you is a part of it.

In 1 Corinthians 12, Paul underscored the main principles that are helpful to each church establishing its mission. He began (verses 1-11) and ended (verses 27-31) the chapter describing how the church members should function using their spiritual gifts in serving. Therefore, Paul instructed the believing community on how the organization should function in order to carry out the mission of the church. The work and ministry of the church should be performed in part through each member using their appointed spiritual gifts. As members see themselves as important, integral parts of their church's mission, they become participants in the ownership of the mission. Members, therefore, are enthusiastic about their service and contributions of time, labor, and money to the church.

Additionally, all members work as a team to accomplish the mission of the church and by creating new converts. The organization creates the template or vehicle by which the work of ministry is accomplished. The Spirit-led multiplicity of individual contributions coordinated by the mission set forth by the church itself creates a wholeness and unity that God uses for soul winning!

The members of the believing community who want to be full, submitted, enthusiastic participants in the vision, purpose, and mission of the church are "followers" of Christ. A fit church has a body led with the Mind of Christ to give them vision and purpose, focus and passion, and mission. The following table summarizes the importance of these biblical metaphors to a faith's fitness. Notice that the bride, branch, and body metaphors express the same ingredients of a fit church described by the Smyrnan, Philadelphian, and Thessalonian churches, but they explain the ingredients a bit more.

Bride = Vision and Purpose:	<u>Love the Lord your God</u>... Matthew 22:37
	Demonstrates attitude, devotion, and discipline
	• Second coming attitude
	• Single-minded focus
	• Suffering devotion
Branch = Focus and Passion:	<u>Love your neighbor as yourself</u>... Matthew 22:39
	Demonstrates duty to stay connected to God and deal with ourselves
	• Surrendered in Christ
	• Steadfast in the Word
	• Serving with fruit
Body = Mission of Ekklesia:	<u>Go and make disciples of all nations</u>... Matthew 28:19-20
	Demonstrates teamwork of community
	• Soul winning, baptizing new converts
	• Serving unto discipleship

A Fit Ekklesia

Church Drivers

Modern-Day Theologians

The cornerstone of Christ has been laid to create the foundation of the fit church. The building blocks are available and on site for construction. Now to complete the build, the mortar is mixed for the fit church to rise. The word apostle in Greek is *apostolos,* meaning "one who is sent forth." The sending is usually an official act sanctioned by a higher spiritual authority or group. The apostolic worker has received a personal, inward commission or calling. God, with the help of mature believers and mentors, equips apostolic workers with the mix of spiritual gifts necessary to do his work. Many apostles are leaders, pastors, and ordained elders within their believing communities. New Testament apostolic workers traveled within a region to proclaim the gospel, support establishing ekklesias, and plant new believing communities.

During the current era of church life, few apostolic workers are sent by their believing communities to plant or to nurture budding ekklesias. Church starts are simply not keeping up with population growth or with church decline. I searched the literature to find authors who have written about the subject of church health and factors that make for an effective church. I wanted to glean wisdom from this dedicated group of people to determine where overlapping ideas or common ground existed among them.

These workers represent the few among us who have accumulated a wealth of understanding and success in leading dynamic churches from a seed they planted or watered and that God grew.[18] Most are ordained clergy who have years of experience living among and managing believers within their ekklesia. Their experience within the Body of Christ and their fulfillment to their own calling leads me to call them modern-day apostles.

I purposely studied books written from the 1990s and the 2000s so that the analysis is in the context of the newly emerged postmodern culture (whether or not those authors recognized this new U.S. church moraine).

My selection criteria were authors who were ordained clergy who viewed the church organization in terms of health. I'm sure that the list is not exhaustive and that I may have inadvertently overlooked some excellent work; however, the review is still representative of this body of wisdom and contributes to our understanding of church wellness.

I found forty books that deal with our topic: factors or characteristics that contribute to make a healthy and effective church. Please see Appendix 1 for the list. In total, the authors discussed twenty-three distinct categories important to church health. The information contained in these books is vast and warrants its own separate discussion; however, to succinctly portray the information for the purpose of discovering theologians' contribution to the optimally fit church, a categorical meta-analysis was performed on these drivers or health factors.

The term "meta-analysis" means that the books were analyzed as a group. I looked specifically at the church health categories that each author believed to be important. This type of analysis places each category in an order of importance, according to the proportion of authors listing an ingredient as important. Looking at these works reveals the traits that theological scholars deem most essential to a church's well-being. Sixteen influential factors were ultimately created from the analysis. The number of books that listed and discussed a particular factor as important to church wellness was tallied as a percentage, and the results are presented as church drivers in the next table.

Church Driver	Percentage
[1]Mind of Christ	87
[2]Leadership	77
Evangelism	77
[3]Discipleship	67
Worship	53
Holy Spirit's Presence	53
[4]Shepherding	51
[5]Service	49
Fellowship	46
Scripture	44
Prayer	36
Structures	23
Preaching (expository)	20
Finance	10
Staff	8
Other	5

Church Drivers That Build a Fit Church

1 vision/purpose, unity, Christian behavior
2 ordained and non-ordained leadership
3 Christian maturity, discipleship, equipping, and discipline
4 focus on membership, pastoral care, and programs
5 ministry (within) and mission (outside the church)

Combining vision, purpose, unity, and Christian behavior categories created the most commonly discussed driver, one that I call the "Mind of Christ." The authors' discussions involving these categories had significant overlap, and when combined, collectively represented the answer to the common colloquialism, "What would Jesus do?" or simply put, "How would Jesus instruct his churches?" As a result, this driver provides great insight into the motivation or heart of a believing community, which represents the essence of Jesus's teachings.

Discussions on leadership tied for second as the most important health factor and centered on the ordained clergy as well as on lay members within the believing community. Though different aspects or descriptions of leadership were discussed, the summation actually represents a leadership style described as "follower leadership." The leadership of both groups is distinctive yet integral to the health of an ekklesia; therefore, I've used the driver *Leadership* to represent the unique importance of these categories.

Evangelism also tied for second. It demonstrates the importance of passing the Kingdom's ecclesial genes to the next generation of believers. By definition, the *Evangelism* driver fulfills the description of church fitness in this model. It represents a church's systematic approach to fulfilling the will of God. (A detailed discussion will follow in the section called "Fit Body.")

I've used the term *Discipleship* to include the authors' discussions of Christian maturity, discipleship, equipping, and discipline. Knowledge of the Word of God, understanding and use of one's spiritual gifts for ministry, consistent and truthful mentoring of the Spirit life, and intimacy with Jesus Christ all represent the ongoing development of a believing community.

More than 50 percent of the discussions surrounded the *Shepherding* driver, which is different from *Discipleship* in that it represents the authors' discussions on caring for or supporting members of the believing community rather than maturing them. Categories such as pastoral care, programs to support congregational care, and focus on the membership were combined to form the *Shepherding* church health factor.

The driver *Service* rounds off the top half of the most important health factors discussed and represents members of the believing community doing ministry within the church or doing mission outside the church. The importance of members participating in the ministries and mission of the church cannot be overstated as a health factor since 50 percent of the authors discussed these categories.

Worship and the presence of the *Holy Spirit* are also included as factors of church health by more than half of the many authors, and both rank high as drivers for health. Most churches place a primary emphasis on worship. But how many churches actually design worship or orchestrate organizational behavior to invite the presence of the Holy Spirit into their assembly on a daily basis? More will be said of these important drivers a little later.

The health factors or drivers that fewer than half our modern-day apostles believe to be important include *Fellowship, Scripture, Prayer, Structures, Preaching,* and *Staff.* The last driver, *Other,* represents discussions that did not fit into any of the above drivers. *Other* represents any undisclosed health factor, which could be important within the context of a believing community. Just because a factor has not been discussed or categorized does not make it any less important to a particular ekklesia.

Though clergy place a high priority on preaching in general, only 20 percent of the discussions surrounded preaching as an important health factor for churches. When preaching was thought to be important, it was specifically expository preaching that became a driver for a healthy church. That is, preaching on a specific text of Scripture, discussing topics therein, and explaining the exact meaning of the passage. Preaching was a central driver for churches during the period of modernity (the peak period of U.S. Christianity), but today it serves a specific function in spiritual education, congregational unity, and leader development.

The ranking of the categories gives leaders an idea of the relative importance of each driver. Leaders can survey the drivers and prioritize the order they wish to emphasize within their Body. This collection of authors has done an excellent job of discussing these drivers in detail. Some of the discussions are quite informative and inspirational. I encourage leaders and emerging leaders to learn as much as possible about these important health factors. Books marked with an asterisk in Appendix 1 represent a good starting point for a more in-depth study.

These biblical drivers are very important to church organizational health, especially the most important category, "Mind of Christ." It is incumbent upon leadership to understand the clinical relevance of these drivers so they can be put into practice.

Academic Researchers

Another valuable source of information available for analysis is that which comes from people who perform academic research with an interest in religious organizations. The results are published in peer-reviewed journals from a variety of disciplines. The authors may or may not be professing Christians. Some are ordained members of the clergy, but many are not. Unlike a book that gives biographical information about the author, journal articles only give academic credentials. Some of the authors are affiliated with seminaries, and a few have strong reputations in the field as ordained clergy. A study is not less valuable because it was performed by a non-Christian or a nominal Christian. That a study is credible because of proper construction, analysis, and conclusion is the basis for consideration as a contribution to understanding church fitness.

Academic peers provide quality control for journal articles. The work of authors must pass a strict review process in order to be published. This helps guarantee a minimum standard of research integrity. Under controlled circumstances, analysis of data should be reproducible, yielding the same results if performed by any researcher. Study limitations are usually disclosed, and public discourses of challenges or questions are usually published as follow-up in the respective journals. Studies are catalogued, open-sourced, and can be retrieved at will.

Scholars use proven research models such as the "social club model" used in sociology to evaluate religious organizations. Many churches behave as a mutual benefit organization whereby the church functions like a social club or volunteer organization: participation is voluntary, sharing is central, and they have the ability to exclude "free-riders."[19]

Academic research requires data. In the studies that will be presented, the data are acquired mostly from two sources: surveys filled out by pastors or church leaders at the request of the researchers, and/or data submitted annually from churches using a denominational database. I will only present those church factors that have been shown under statistical analysis to be significantly associated with church health. These factors are called "independent variables in research." This type of research suggests whether independent variables will have an impact on or can be used to predict a change in the metric under study: the dependent variable. The most common dependent variable available for assessing church health is a measurement of growth.

Since the definition of church fitness is creating new converts or passing on the DNA of the gospel into new generations, church growth is a fair approximation of church fitness. It may not be the best dependent variable, but it is one that is easily measurable and that is the most commonly used among researchers. Perhaps a better measurement for church fitness would be the number of professions of faith in Christ (at home and abroad on the mission field) or the number of new churches birthed, because these measurements suggest new growth within a church.

I want to discuss one last point about these academic studies. Beyond the independent church factors that are associated with growth, statistical analysis demonstrates that most church studies have other factors that also account for changes in growth that cannot be explained (this is called "R-squared" in the field of statistics). To researchers, unexplained factors are the immeasurable, intangible, or unaccounted-for factors that are called "noise." For example, it is difficult for researchers to quantify the presence of the Holy Spirit in any given church. In fact, some academicians only want to deal with measurable variables and voice no public opinion about the belief in or importance of the Holy Spirit in religious organizations.

The Christian researcher, however, recognizes that the presence of the Holy Spirit may be one of the immeasurable forces that contributes greatly to an ekklesia's fitness level. In an academic study performed by Simon Medcalfe and Cecil Sharp, we freely admit to the limitations of academic models successfully describing the influence of the Holy Spirit on a church.[20]

> Certain intangible measures, like ecclesia—the gathering of people for the spiritual purposes of worship, relationship, and discipleship using the Holy Spirit—are unique to Protestant religious construct and to local church health. The ability of economics to bridge the chasm between tangible measures and less tangible ecclesial measures may be another contributor to the low R squared values among these types of religious studies.

Finding any statistically significant association among independent variables demonstrates an important strength of association with growth. Though academic research does a poor job of directly measuring the spiritual aspects of a believing community, important church factors including indirect spiritual factors can still be gleaned from this type of research.

I searched the literature for studies on church growth and found thirty academic sources published by twenty-one different groups of researchers from three different countries. Because of the unique perspective of these academic studies, I've included research from the modern and postmodern church eras between the years of 1972 and 2012. A list of these studies with their corresponding journals and authors is shared in Appendix 2. I'm sure the list is not exhaustive, and some well-structured studies may have inadvertently been left out of the analysis. The majority were published in professional peer-review journals with appropriate statistical analysis. The fields of religion, sociology, economics, and mathematics were represented, and at least seven separate sects of Christianity were used in the research.

For each study, I have listed the major significant independent variables or church factors that statistically explained changes in church growth (the dependent variable). These influencers of church growth along with their academic studies are listed in the appendix "Church Factors from Academic Studies." Again, an exhaustive discussion about the studies will not be given here. Every study is well-written and contributes to the model of a fit church.

Leaders should review the church factors in the table and select specific articles of interest to read and review. Group discussions could be designed around the review of these articles. Church leaders could learn valuable lessons about different aspects of church life.

To help conceptualize these major influences on growth, church factors were put into one of the following specific categories: context, program, identity, or process. A brief discussion follows.

Context

Context helps us understand the external, environmental, societal, and national circumstances that influence church growth. At the time of our country's founding, there were only a handful of religious choices. By 1990, American congregations had evolved (and fragmented) to form more than 2,500 religious sects in more than 300,000 religious congregations that made a combined annual revenue of over $50 billion.[21, 22] Multiple studies demonstrate that the sectarian groups (Adventist, Jehovah's Witnesses, Church of Jesus Christ of Latter-day Saints, Church of God, etc.) and the conservative U.S. Protestant faiths (Baptist, Presbyterian Church PC, New Evangelical Movement, Independent, organic, home, etc.) are on the rise, while U.S. mainline and liberal faith groups (Lutheran, United Methodist, Presbyterian USA, United Church of Christ, Episcopal, Catholic, etc.) are on the decline.

In our recent study of one of the largest conferences in the United Methodist Church, 46 percent of churches had a mean rate of membership decline of 13 percent during the three-year study period. Only 54 percent of churches were stable or growing somewhat. It seems as though local communities pick the winners and losers based upon a church's ability to provide important religious resources. The proportion of churches that are successful in reaching the next generation of believers either *de novo* or by planting new churches is less than five percent. In the same conference, only three new church starts occurred during the three-year study period.[23]

Research has demonstrated that conservative churches grow at the expense of liberal churches. That trend is accelerating in the postmodern age. Theological conservatism creates a type of "strictness" that increases levels of commitment among members who are willing to invest time, labor, and financial resources into their religious community.

The source of conservative faith growth is intriguing. Switchers (members who switch their membership from one church to another) explain 70 percent of conservative church growth—not converts to the gospel of Jesus Christ, even as the population of non-believers has increased! Though some switchers are free-riding circulating saints, most are transformed, submitted Christians who've become frustrated with their local church and seek to practice their faith in a significant missional context.

The offspring of church members, "reproducers," who also join, account for another 20 percent. "Converters," nonbelievers who give their life to Jesus Christ and join, make up just 10 percent of conservative church growth. In the 1970s, 69 percent of children raised in the church returned as adults to the church, compared to only 17 percent today. The ability to reproduce new converts is critical to revival growth in the Kingdom and prevents extinction.[24,25] A shift in the membership moraine has occurred.

Laurence Iannaccone describes strictness as, "demands for complete loyalty, unwavering belief, and rigid adherence to a distinctive lifestyle."[26] Money, time in Christian maturity and ministry, and effort in shepherding and missions are member resources and valued commodities. Strict conservative denominations have a more homogenous community with a common vision. They receive a higher percentage of their members' incomes, and what is lacking in financial resources tends to be exacted in a higher amount of time and labor.

Conservative Christian constituents are more balanced in their giving of time and money. The decline in mainline denominations compared to the increase in strict denominations is partly explained by radically different amounts of time, effort, and money that each demand and receive from its members.

Small churches tend to grow to an optimal size. Only a small number grow into large congregations. An exception to this rule is some of the large independent metropolitan churches (with 300 or more members). Factors that influence church size include leadership's ability to handle economies of scale, organizational function, staffing models, facility stewardship, and church satellite management. Traditional churches differ from these large, growing postmodern churches in that the marginal benefit of adding an additional member seems to decrease as membership increases mainly because of the increasing marginal cost of that member (including the loss of time, labor, and/or money due to congestion, and the tendency for members to attend without giving financially).[27]

Clergy age is another contextual variable that affects growth. Clergy age has increased dramatically and keeps pace with our aging Baby Boomer population. Younger clergy understand and connect with young people, which draws a greater number of like-minded people. The paucity of young ordained elders, clergy, and priests is a significant factor in church growth. In 2009, one mainline denomination reported that the number of active elders under thirty-five years of age was only 5 percent. Practicing elders between thirty-five and fifty-four represent 47 percent, and the largest group, the fifty-five to seventy-two age cohort, make up 48 percent. The median and average age of elders were both fifty-four, and the average age for deacons was fifty-one. Lovett H. Weems and Ann A. Michel, in *Why Young Clergy Matter*, state: "Young clergy also have certain advantages in reaching out to their own generation. They are more likely to speak the language of an emerging generation whose world view and communication modes differ from those of their parents' generation." Indeed, they are well suited to the task of church planting, and they bring a fresh perspective and enthusiasm to the ministry. A wave of retiring senior clergy will leave a paucity of leadership and a missed opportunity for leadership succession.[28]

Program

Organizational structure, planning, and activities are three variables that make up the programmatic component of growth. The most important elements are small groups and a menu of differing programs, regardless of congregation size. Believers are able to connect, live, and relate through intimate gatherings. Churches with a higher number of program offerings attract more people to participate in groups. When those functions have an educational bent for maturing believers, a youth or children orientation, and a small size, then others want to join the experience. An extensive menu of programs is likely to reach a broader range of interests within the congregation or local community.

Worship style is also important for growth. A higher percent of congregations who describe their last worship service as being "filled with God's presence" participated in an alternative style of worship. It is one of the strongest catalysts for spiritual vitality and growth. Sixty-four percent of congregations that started an alternative worship experience grew 2 percent or more over a five-year period from 2005 to 2010! However, during the same period, only 12 percent of congregations added that style of worship. Interestingly, old-line faith groups (mostly synonymous with mainline) are now accelerating with the change to or addition of an alternative worship style, so this should increase their growth.

Identity

The beliefs and values of each local church, despite denominational affiliation, factor significantly into growth. We've already shown that theologically conservative churches with strict beliefs grow better than churches that have loosely held beliefs. Local faith communities, regardless of denominational affiliation, with spiritual practices like corporate prayer, singing, or reading of Scripture that welcome the Holy Spirit in worship, promote increased worship attendance and membership. An increasing worship attendance to member ratio seems to demonstrate enthusiasm among participants. Churches that are characterized by racial and gender diversity also tend to thrive. Homogeneous congregations dominated by white participants or men do not grow as well. Groups that place a premium on friendships and caring for children and youth also grow.

Women are extremely important to the Kingdom as well as to church health. A 2011 study has found that church attendance, Bible reading, Sunday school attendance, and volunteering among women has dropped at church by about 10 percent since 1991.[29] Women tend to be the managers of their families. When female members attend worship and become full participants in the life of a church, their children follow and growth occurs.

Process

Churches that are strong in the areas of leadership, decision-making, problem-solving, and conflict management perform better than churches without these traits. These factors seem to increase organizational identification and member commitment, which in turn does three things. First, members believe in and accept the communities' goals, values, and style. Second, members are willing to exert effort in the form of time, labor, and money to the community. Third, members want to maintain their membership and connection with the organization.

When leaders focus on having a positive outlook, increasing spiritual vitality, and transforming members into enthusiasts (full participants), members respond with increased participation. Communities with a self-focus, mainly on their own faith, worship style, or personal growth, or with conflict in worship, leadership, or finances, experience the inverse of growth: decline!

The only financial influencers that have been strong enough to demonstrate growth are pastor compensation and identified givers' contributions. Congregations with higher pastor compensation grew more significantly than those with lower compensation. This association does not explain why the relationship holds. It may be that the best clergy are highly valued and paid according to their performance and giftedness.

The majority of church revenue comes from both member and non-member giving. Some visitors do not identify themselves when they give to a church. Members, on the other hand, give a prescribed amount regularly (we call these "pledge givers"), or they donate independent of a pledge ("identified givers"). It has been shown that members of conservative faiths are more likely to vote on their agreement with the direction of the church with their feet by either staying or leaving, whereas members of mainline denominations tend to vote with their monetary giving. Increases in identified giving are associated with church growth.

The understanding of academic drivers for congregational growth reduces misinformation circulating about religious studies and helps leaders focus on the factors that contribute to church wellness. Most of the church factors obtained from researchers fit into at least one of the church drivers derived from modern-day theological authors. Integrating the two perspectives gives a more complete picture of the factors that influence church wellness and growth. The mixture creates the mortar that helps build the fit church. These determinants are displayed in the next table, Academic Factors That Drive Church Growth.

Church Drivers	**Academic Factors**
1 Mind of Christ	Conservative sects Denominational affiliation Independent churches Religious resources New Evangelical Movement Conservative beliefs Traditional beliefs Strict beliefs Absence of conflict (worship, leadership, finances) Losing members (without same vision)
2 Leadership	Conservative beliefs Traditional beliefs Strict beliefs Strict beliefs eliminate "free riders" Small groups Church school size Education emphasis Extensiveness of programs Contemporary worship Positive outlook for future Leadership/vision/mission/purpose/training Increasing spiritual vitality Small groups build commitment Organizational commitment/identification Making converts into enthusiasts/stem losses Pastor compensation per member Absence of conflict (worship, leadership, finances)
Evangelism	Newer worshipers/percentage of new members Worship attendance and contributions Incr. ratio of attendance at worship/member Female members Absence of predominantly white members
3 Discipleship	Small groups Education emphasis Church participation Worship attendance and contributions Incr. ratio of attendance at worship/member Use of spiritual gifts to build commitment Beliefs lead to commitment Making converts into enthusiasts/stem losses Identified givers in contributions
Worship	Contemporary worship Presence of Holy Spirit in worship Spiritual practices

Holy Spirit	Contemporary worship Church participation Worship attendance and contributions Incr. ratio of attendance at worship/member Absence of predominantly white members Use of spiritual gifts to build commitment Increasing spiritual vitality Making converts into enthusiasts/stem losses
4 Shepherding	Small groups Children/youth focus/programs Church participation Caring for children/youth
5 Services	Use of spiritual gifts to build commitment Caring for children/youth Specialty programs Children/youth focus/program Education emphasis
Fellowship	Small groups Female members Worship attendance and contributions
Word of God	Conservative beliefs Traditional beliefs Strict beliefs Spiritual practices Church participation
Prayer	Spiritual practices Church participation
Structures	Member resources
Preaching (expository)	Conservative beliefs, traditional beliefs Strict beliefs Strict beliefs eliminate "free riders" Presence of Holy Spirit in worship Worship attendance and contributions
Finance	Worship attendance and contributions Identified givers in contributions Pastor compensation per member
Staff	Church school size, education emphasis Extensiveness of programs Contemporary worship Children/youth focus/programs Specialty programs

Academic Factors That Drive Church Growth

1 vision/purpose, unity, Christian behavior
2 ordained and non-ordained leadership
3 Christian maturity, discipleship, equipping, and discipline
4 focus on membership, pastoral care and programs
5 ministry (within) and mission (outside the church)

Four different attributes contribute to church health: the Word of God, the experience and tradition of modern-day theologians, and the research of scholars. Spiritual leaders should use Scripture to develop the ingredients of a healthy church and fit ekklesia. Modern-day theologians offer a hierarchy of factors for leaders to prioritize and build up using researched variables that are known to generate growth.

In the next section, we'll apply the knowledge from these fitness drivers to create a fit Body and a fitness lifestyle for our healthy churches.

"For I know the plans I have for you," declares the Lord,
"plans to prosper you and not to harm you,
plans to give you hope and a future."
Jeremiah 29:11

Fitness Moment

- Jesus Christ and the Word of God using the ingredients of church health modeled by New Testament churches are the central drivers of church health.
- Biblical metaphors like that of the Bride, the Branch, and the Body give insight into a fit ekklesia. They model the Mind of Christ.
- A categorical analysis of books written by mostly ordained clergy suggests a hierarchy of organizational drivers for use by wellness-oriented church leaders.
- Categories that demand the most emphasis include the Mind of Christ (vision/purpose/unity/behavior), evangelism, leadership (ordained and non-ordained), discipleship, worship, and the Holy Spirit.

- Academic researchers contribute drivers for church growth, and these drivers can be used along with the drivers in the categorical format to build a strategic plan for drawing new members or for improving fitness.
- Follow the prescription for renewal and recommitment to build upon your healthy foundation.

Renew and Recommit

Sig: *follow the instructions*
Refill(s): *prn – as needed*
Comments: *No substitutions permitted*

May your hearts be fully committed to the Lord our God,
to live by his decrees and obey his commands.[30]

This prescription is all about regeneration and new growth. As leaders, we have confessed, repented, and turned away from our sin. In renewal, the underlying granulation tissue of the heart regenerates. This new growth will help the body rediscover the meaning of true fitness and its role in establishing a fitness lifestyle. The Old Testament books of Ezra and Nehemiah are about God renewing his errant people. Ezra tells the story about the return of the exiles from Babylon, the rebuilding of the temple, and the spiritual restoration of God's people. Nehemiah is about the rebuilding of the walls of Jerusalem, as well as the spiritual renewal of God's people.

The story in Ezra begins with the initial return of the dedicated remnant of his children. God can build upon a remnant of committed followers. In the Revelation churches, a remnant of believers demonstrated either faith or works while the rest of the church members were criticized. Ezra's temple restoration project took twenty-three years (538 B.C. to 515 B.C.) to complete in the midst of much opposition and many obstacles.[31] He commissioned leaders and restored his people to spiritually proper worship and godly living. Do you think it will be easy to restore your church in renewal?

Spiritual renewal is difficult because man wants to control the process. Renewal requires spiritual power to overcome the pull of the world and the ungodly forces that want to assimilate us away from God's holy Church.[32] "Do not conform to the pattern of this world, but be transformed by the renewing of your mind. Then you will be able to test and approve what God's will is—his good, pleasing and perfect will."[33] Renewal only comes from God's grace and his mighty power. Human effort doesn't bring renewal. Only God can promise restoration, and it comes through his Word. Leaders must get themselves and their churches back to daily Scripture reading, devotion, and prayer.

When the Eastern tribes returned to Jordan, Joshua gathered and presented the leadership from all the tribes of Israel to God. It was time for their covenant renewal.[34] He didn't gather the entire nation of Israel, but the leaders of each tribe. He told them before God, "Now therefore fear the Lord and serve him in sincerity and in faithfulness.... But as for me and my house, we will serve the Lord."[35] Should the leaders of your church come together for a covenant renewal with God? A proclamation, a joint decision, to serve him sincerely is an important step in faith fitness.

The leaders of Israel and the leaders of the Revelation churches had a responsibility to the Lord. Jesus's words to each Revelation church teach us that God measures the quality of our collective response in his churches. Our ekklesias are accountable to him, and his measuring stick for quality is love.[36] Renewal is necessary to sustain our churches' love for the Lord, love for ourselves, and love of our neighbors. Jesus knows that love is more than belief; it is action. Jesus gave the apostle Peter a call to action when he reinstated Peter after he denied Jesus three times. As you and your church arise to regain your footing, Jesus is already challenging your body with a call to action. His instructions are clear: "Do you love me more than these… Follow me!"[37]

Renewal is an important step in becoming a wellness-oriented church, and renewal leads directly to recommitment. We have one last confession to make, the confession of faith. We have lost our connection to the head.[38] To truly restore our fortunes, we need to restore Jesus to the headship of our church, his rightful place.

We are reminded there is one Lord, one faith, one body, one Spirit, and one God and Father of all.[39] We need to stop believing in our different doctrines and tenets and believe in the Lord. "What is all striving, could it ever encompass a world, but a half-finished work if one does not know thee: thee the One, who art one thing and who art all!"[40] By returning Christ to our true center, our true north, and our core belief, we are recommitting to a new birth for our ekklesia and a living hope.[41]

Every apostolic fellowship is a fellowship of truth. Under heavy persecution, the early church needed words that would sum up their purpose. The creeds or confessions of faith became their banner of commitment. The most acclaimed creed became known as the Apostles' Creed. In some churches today, the words are recited during worship services, but the creed carries no meaning to people who know little about a suffering faith.

In Jesus's time, pious Jews also daily recited a creed known as the Jewish confession of faith, the Shema.[42] *Shema* means "to hear" in Hebrew. In the New Testament, Jesus answered a Sadducee's question and taught his followers the new importance of the Shema ritual: "Hear, O Israel: The Lord our God, the

Lord is one. Love the Lord your God with all your heart and with all your soul and with all your mind and with all your strength."[43]

Jesus is saying that not only should we turn away from the world and our sin, but we must also recommit to our Savior. Reread the confession, and this time put your name in place of the word "Israel." Reread the confession another time, putting the name of your church in place of the word Israel. As leaders within our own ekklesias, do we make decisions based upon this creed?

If our fellowship is to join the community of fit athletes known as "a royal priesthood, a holy nation, God's special possession," then we must take this confession of faith seriously.[44] As a member of this universal body of Christ, confession of our sins and confession of our faith in Jesus Christ are the only fertilizers that may save the barren fig tree.[45] It is impossible to live for Christ without first having died with Christ.

Have we reached the tipping point in believing that it is possible to accept Christ without forsaking the world? While kneeling, the church leaders must acknowledge the words of James: "Know ye not that the friendship of the world is enmity with God? Whosoever therefore will be a friend of the world is the enemy of God,"[46] and, "If any man love the world, the love of the Father is not in him."[47] We must not allow the world to call us out of our churches.

In the forty days after his resurrection, Jesus appeared to many early believers, including the disciples. On one occasion at daybreak, Jesus found that seven of his disciples had returned to the Sea of Galilee. What were they doing there? They had returned to their first calling, the only other thing they knew: fishing. The story of Peter on the shore is one of the most compelling stories of recommitment.

In the heat of the moment, with two outs in the bottom of the ninth inning, Peter stepped away from the batter's box and went fishing. A coach once told me that even great players rarely rise to the occasion; instead, they revert back to their training. That's why training is so important! Peter reverted back to his training as a fisherman.[48]

Jesus knew where to find his band of brothers, and he knows where to find you. Unfortunately, too often he finds us in the world, not seeking his heart. That's where Jesus found Peter, on the shore with a broken heart. The last time they fished together, the nets needed mending after their large catch, and the heart of Peter became closely knit with Jesus.[49] This time, the large catch did not break the nets, but it was Peter's heart that required mending. Jesus reinstated Peter as a fisher of men after asking him three times, "do you love me?"[50] With each response, the hole in Peter's heart became healed. Peter could now resume his proper training as a submitted follower. As believers, we know that Peter did rise to the occasion; he carried out the work of Christ by providing the fruitful work of spreading the gospel and building up Jesus's church.[51]

There is a clear line of demarcation between the flesh and the Spirit. That which is born of the flesh is flesh and that which is born of the Spirit is spirit.[52] Commitment is choosing to live in accordance with the Spirit and having the mind set on what the Spirit desires.[53] Committing to Christ means that every decision of the church is based upon the Mind of Christ, not members within the body.

Since we are members of one body, when the body has its heart on Christ and its mind on things above, the body will enjoy the peace of Christ and a unity of Spirit.[54] Our recommitment to Christ gives a restored church the FAITH to run the race: **F**ollowers **A**rise with the **I**ndwelling Spirit and **T**ransformed **H**earts.

5

FIT BODY

Therefore, I urge you, brothers and sisters, in view of God's mercy
to offer your bodies as a living sacrifice, holy and pleasing to God—
this is your true and proper worship.
Romans 12:1

Brian is my son, and Carleton is my son-in-law. Upon arriving at the CrossFit® gym, Carleton scanned the list of names and found Brian's time for the "WOD," Workout of the Day. "Ouch, that'll be a tough time to beat on today's workout," said Carleton, who is a fit twenty-nine-year-old. The workout included ten high intensity physical skills, including tire lifts, pull-ups, and a series of sprints. Upon completing the WOD, Carleton couldn't wait to text his time to Brian, who had barely eclipsed his friend. Brian immediately called Carleton back, and they discussed the WOD for some time while they laughed and poked fun at each other. Brian got Carleton into CrossFit. "Now he's very competitive," said Brian. Both friends are hooked.

CrossFit is a strength and conditioning brand that promotes daily workouts in a community environment of like-minded fitness enthusiasts. Greg and Lauren Glassman started this virtual brand of fitness centers. The workouts are carefully crafted to build proficiency in areas of stamina, strength, flexibility, and power.

Like many Millennials and GenXers, Brian and Carleton go to the gym at least five times a week to work out simultaneously with others who form a community. CrossFit offers participants the chance to build relationships, which often strengthens their motivation to work out. Plus, it becomes more difficult to fall into a rut of doing the same exercises, which can become unrewarding emotionally and physiologically. Boring workouts have been transformed into a community sport, which makes the WOD fun. Additional relationships are built by talking to others with the same interest in health and nutrition.

The CrossFit culture builds community when members post comments as a response to sharing tips on nutrition and proper workout techniques. This input by fellow enthusiasts is valued as insightful and inspiring.[1] An energetic culture of devotees is created to share the lifestyle of physical fitness.

The word "gymnasium" is derived from the Greek word *gumnazo,* which means "exercise." Gyms or fitness centers like CrossFit focus mainly on physical training. Paul says, "For physical training is of some value, but godliness has value for all things, holding promise for both the present life and the life to come."[2] He also says to "train yourself to be godly."[3]

As Paul's words suggest, the world of fitness training offers useful metaphors for living the Christian life. Jesus means for us to be in continual spiritual training.[4] Christians within the early Church were committed to "the Way" as a lifestyle. During our postmodern epoch, the divide between Christians and nonbelievers is so great that simply issuing an invitation to attend church can be a challenge. Are we even prepared to engage our neighbors in love? Fit followers are the elite spiritual athletes within our churches. Being a mature follower means that we mentor younger believers in an intentional systematic process that is engaging and fulfilling so that people like Carleton and Brian are as excited to learn about Jesus and enjoy the challenge of spiritual training in community as they are about CrossFit.

When a church is healthy, then it will "worship the Lord in the beauty of holiness"[5] and pass on the Christian heritage to the next generation of followers.[6] Spiritual fitness for the follower has a parallel to training for the sports athlete. It is the duty of the leadership, ordained and non-ordained, to construct inviting processes and structures that function like a spiritual training site and a holy respite for young believers in training.

The descriptor already used for this fit church archetype is "follower training site." Much like the CrossFit training center, the fts becomes the ekklesia's vehicle to fulfill its purpose by working in community to reproduce fit followers so the church can accomplish its vision. Do you remember the different facilities used to describe the dysfunctional Revelation churches—corporate, collegiate, civic club, city council, and country club? A fit church will function as a type of spiritual fitness center, a temple for spiritual development, where the culture of the church is immersed in training members in a lifestyle of following Jesus.

State-of-the-art fitness centers are not about their buildings. They are functional facilities that afford fitness-conscious people the opportunity to get into shape. The fitness brands that are the most successful today are those that offer quality training and community workout routines, not those with fancy facilities designed for the uncommitted. Please understand that the physical assets within your church facility are not a limitation for becoming a spiritual fitness center.

Fit Leaders

In Paul's letters to the Corinthian church he is beseeching the people to work together, overcome conflict, and exercise the gifts of the Spirit. Paul managed the early church much like leaders should be managing their churches today.

He wanted the early Christians to develop into worthy followers, and our goal as leaders should be the same. He told the Corinthians that God's purpose is to make believers godly.[7]

Healthy congregations who want to become wellness-oriented must first have fit leaders who are Christ-centered and committed to creating a facility that can achieve the fit church archetype. Leaders who are committed to Christ and have his heart will understand their community. Their focus will be on the next generation. With a fit heart, churches can build strategies to attract people who are interested in their vision, mission, and purpose. Church leaders should work together to create a facility that trains members into worthy followers who build up the Body.

Spiritual fitness for a church leader is not that different from fitness for the sports athlete. Using this analogy can help leaders understand the interrelated functions within the Body of Christ. The categorical analysis has already established the most important drivers for church health. The following table, Body Building, uses the leading church drivers (taken from the Wellness Toolbox) to demonstrate this important relationship. Leaders can better create an optimally fit Body by understanding the corollary between church fitness drivers and the human body.

Fitness Driver	Human Body
Jesus – Mind of Christ *	Head
Holy Spirit	Heartbeat and breath
Leadership, Ordained	Central nervous system
Preaching	Messaging
Staff	Supporting nerve units
Leadership, Laity	Cardiovascular system
Evangelism	Reproductive system

Body Building

* (vision, purpose, mission, unity, Christian behavior)

The Mind of Christ

We've already discussed that Jesus Christ is the head of the Church.[8] Therefore, he is the head of the Body within every Christian church. The most significant driver in the fitness toolbox was the Mind of Christ: the vision, purpose, mission, unity, and Christian behavior of an ekklesia. In addition to explaining the ingredients of the healthy church, the biblical metaphors about the Bride, Branch, and Body also demonstrate the Mind of Christ. Let's highlight the importance of this part of the fit Body and consider how it can be specifically tailored to every church.

Purpose

The purpose of all churches should be the same: to pass on their beliefs and practices to the next generation. The philosopher Soren Kierkegaard says, "The thing is to understand myself, to see what God really wishes me to do... to find the idea for which I can live and die." The third cardinal principal of Peter Drucker, the influential business management consultant, is to "work only on things that will make a great deal of difference if you succeed." The key for your church in this passage is finding your "one thing," your purpose. An organization's purpose is member-oriented and provides motivation for members to work as a team. The purpose tells "why" its members are motivated or dedicated to the task at hand.

Organizational purpose can be written in the form of a purpose statement. Do you recall the story of the three bricklayers?

> A gentleman saw three men laying bricks. He approached the first and asked, "*What are you doing?*"
> Annoyed, the first man answered, "*What does it look like I'm doing? I'm laying bricks!*"
> He walked over to the second bricklayer and asked the same question.
> The second man responded, "*Oh, I'm making a living.*"

He then asked the third bricklayer the same question, *"What are you doing?"*

The third looked up, smiled, and said, *"I'm building a cathedral."*

It is important for people to know the higher purpose or reason they work on a project. When written in the form of a purpose statement, its members can be reminded about making a difference in their work. The organizational purpose statement reminds individual members of the larger project they're working toward. The focus rests on the worker or member. The purpose of a church can be explicitly expressed and clearly understood by all. It gives deep personal meaning to the doers. It is something that everyone can believe in and support.

The best writing on the subject of "church purpose" comes from Rick Warren's *The Purpose Driven Church*. Warren, the pastor of Saddleback Community Church, masterfully outlines a process for defining, communicating, organizing, and applying your purpose. The book is a must-read for church leaders. Please take the time to read and study the material in his book. Saddleback's purpose statement includes the five key words that summarize Christ's five purposes for his church:

To bring people to Jesus and **membership** in his family, develop them to Christ-like **maturity**, and equip them for their **ministry** in the church and life **mission** in the world, in order to **magnify** God's name.[9]

Notice that the purposes are stated as results and arranged into the sequential process that encourages participation by every member. Warren states that the heart of a purpose-driven church is to "focus on growing people with a process," not with programs. Aligning the mission and vision with God's purpose for your church will have great Kingdom impact.

Now that we have some understanding of the importance of our churches' "purpose," let's distinguish purpose from vision and mission. As we've already discussed, the concept of spiritual fitness means passing on the saving knowledge of the gospel to other generations, not just our own. Paul and Apollos were two leaders in the early church. A division occurred because they seemed to have different purposes. Paul makes it clear that in a church, we work together; we plant the seed, Apollos waters it, and God makes it grow.[10] If our church is to play a significant role in the Kingdom, we must reach our children's children. We must run this race, not for souls "just like us," but for the souls of God's desire. This distinction is the key for your ekklesia to regenerate new enthusiasts; otherwise, you will continue faltering with business as usual. Leaders that can communicate the church's purpose create a unity among its followers.

Vision

Most churches have a statement, motto, or logo that members would recognize. It may be displayed on the church's letterhead, flyers, bulletin, website, or any regular member publication. Usually these communications are meant to demonstrate a mission statement. A church's vision, however, is much more elusive.

I recently asked a friend who is a leader at her church to pass out a blank sheet of paper to everyone in attendance at her next church executive meeting. Next, she was to ask everyone present to write the church's vision down on the paper. She reported that no one was able to. No one knew the church's vision, not even the pastor. Was it because they did not have a vision? Perhaps the very concept of vision is illusory or confusing?

To make the somewhat abstract concept of "vision" more manageable, I'll define it as a ten-year goal that expresses the direction an organization would like to head and inspires enthusiasm, sets standards of excellence, and reflects the uniqueness of the organization. It does not need to be linear or concretely measurable. Instead, it describes *what* an organization is striving for and *where* an organization is going. It is appropriate for the vision to be pie-in-the-sky dreaming!

The vision for an organization serves the same function as the rudder of a boat; it helps take your assembly in a desired direction. A notable Yogi Berra(ism) is, "If you don't know where you're going, you might end up someplace else." It is the duty of the captain (in this case, mainly ordained leadership) to direct the rudder from the helm. The captain's compass is the Word of God. Without anyone on the bridge to man the helm, the ship of your ekklesia will drift aimlessly in the ocean.

A vision is not a prophecy about the future. It does not tell you how your church will get there. The vision tells members about their common goals. Vision allows us to really see where we're going. A vision allows the church to use information, knowledge, and wisdom to dream. Not all members or leaders are gifted at dreaming, though; every believer is appointed a different measure of faith. Anyone can shoot in the dark. A visionary can shoot at something that no one else can see and hits it! The greatest visionary is Jesus Christ. He gave us two visionary statements, the Great Commandment and the Great Commission, which summarize his vision for the church. The Great Commandment urges us to: " 'Love the Lord your God with all your heart and with all your soul and with all your mind… Love your neighbor as yourself.' All the Law and the Prophets hang on these two commandments."[11] The Great Commission tells us to, "Go and make disciples of all nations, baptizing them in the name of the Father and of the Son and of the Holy Spirit, and teaching them to obey everything I have commanded you."[12]

Most denominations or independent church bodies have a written vision statement similar to the ones above. Our problem is not that we lack a vision, but that we do not know it, believe it, or use it as leverage to accomplish God's will for our church. For the renewing assembly, a vision should be bold and complementary to the vision of Christ.

In order to accomplish our dreams, though, we must stay grounded as we strive for an improved level of fitness. We have many members, but few enthusiasts or fit followers in our community. The Commitment Diagram (Member Enthusiasm) discussed earlier in the chapter "Understanding Fitness" helps to explain how the flux of people inside and outside the ekklesia results in fit followers. Nonbelievers are converted to the gospel and become enthusiasts for Christ, committed followers who generously give their time, labor, money, and service. More importantly, enthusiasts are "fit" believers because they are devoted adherents to the purpose, vision, and mission of the church. Notice that believers can increase their level of commitment within the church until they become fit followers (enthusiasts), too.

It is essential that restored churches build up fit followers. The harvest is plentiful, but the enthusiasts are few.[13] God wants his Word to spread and the number of fit followers to increase as rapidly as possible.[14] Every assembly has the full complement of spiritual gifts. God awards talents according to the faith fitness of every ekklesia. Grow your level of fitness so that your ekklesia doesn't become an irrelevant player in Kingdom life. Followers need to be reminded of their church's vision. Leadership is responsible for that task.

Let's see how a church's vision can be accomplished.

Mission

If Jesus is the Great Visionary, then we in the church are his missionaries. We carry out the vision and translate it into action. The mission of the church is to fulfill the purpose of the church. Mission and purpose are two sides of the same coin. Most organizations write a mission statement to give employees a linear, measurable understanding of their target. It is written from the organization's perspective, whereas the purpose is written from the member's perspective. The mission answers the "how" question; it articulates how to carry out the vision, usually in a time frame of three years or less.

The difference between vision and mission can be further explained with a boat analogy. A boat captain uses the rudder to move in a certain direction: the "vision" of the church. The kind of boat is specific to the mission of the church. If the mission requires a tour boat, we wouldn't use a tugboat or a dredging barge. Leadership is responsible for providing the mission or type of boat that will be used to carry out the vision.

The McDonald's Corporation's mission statement is "to be our customers' favorite place and way to eat and drink. Being the favorite means McDonald's centers on an exceptional customer experience—people, products, place, price and promotion."[15] There are hundreds of fast food restaurants, but McDonald's chooses to accomplish their vision through their customer experience. Their brand of happiness is evident in children wanting to come back for more. In addition, they have an ambitious statement on their corporate website that focuses on good food, good people, and good community.

The brief mission statement at my church is, "Welcome * Win * Grow * Send." Wherever our enthusiasts meet people, we invite and make them welcome at our church. Visitors are then won by the saving knowledge of Jesus Christ and become members of his church. Next, we attempt to equip, disciple, and grow believers into maturity. Finally, believers are encouraged to live according to God's call and his will in their lives.

Notice that both statements reveal more about the target or customer, rather than individuals already in the organization. This is typical of a mission statement; it focuses on the one being served.

Vision, mission, or purpose statements can be written concisely so that they become constant reminders to organizational members; some statements adorn business cards, T-shirts, hats, or bracelets! Try it at your church.

Getting a church's membership to understand and own the organizational purpose is what branding experts call "tactical internal branding." The organizational brand will expand externally as each church accomplishes its vision while exercising the mission in the lives of people. The church's mission becomes the full satisfying expression of the love its followers have for Jesus Christ and their neighbors in the world. And with these changes a church is on its way to becoming wellness-oriented.

Holy Spirit

Most would agree that one of the most important organs in the human body is the heart. Without a heartbeat, there is no life. A birth certificate is based upon the beating heart, a live birth. A death certificate is based upon the cessation of the beating heart. A naturally healthy heart functions for the fullness of a lifetime. The Holy Spirit gives churches its heartbeat. The heart of a church may be its lay leadership and its members, but the functionality, performance, and pulse of the heart is dependent upon the presence of the Holy Spirit. Without the Holy Spirit, a church is dead.

The heart is a remarkable organ that must adapt in order to meet the demands of the body. It is integral to the body's cardiovascular system. Everyone can agree that oxygen and nutrients are necessary for human life. When the muscles exercise or work, the heart beats faster and harder to deliver more oxygen and nutrients. Over time, this process actually strengthens the heart by making it more flexible and adaptable, improving its cardiovascular shape. As a body increases its fitness, the heart increases and sustains the body's needs. A sedentary person with little activity or exercise has a smaller, less flexible or adaptable heart than an active person. This leads to a poor cardiovascular condition that puts him at risk for many diseases.

A fit athlete has the capacity to extract and deliver oxygen to his body in a very efficient manner (a concept called "VO_2"). This ability is a learned physiologic response from years of training and allows for optimal performance. Muscles only work when they are supplied oxygen and nutrients. The more expertly the heart pumps blood to the muscles, the more efficiency and power results.

The Holy Spirit is as essential to life in a church as a heart is for the human body. On the day of Pentecost, the Holy Spirit came with a sound like the wind, and all that were present were filled.[16] The disciples became empowered to serve after they were filled with the Holy Spirit. The early church started after Pentecost, and today's churches require the Holy Spirit for proper function. A fit church is as dependent on the Holy Spirit as an elite athlete is dependent on a fit heart. Without the Holy Spirit, churches are polluting their sanctuaries and limiting their vitality.

As described in the chapter "Understanding Fitness," Christ criticized five of the Revelation churches for having dysfunctional hearts. Recall that the church of Ephesus had a compassionless spirituality with an asynchronous heart; Pergamum had a conspicuous spirituality with a swollen heart; Thyatira had a counterfeit spirituality with a dilated heart; Sardis had a compromising spirituality with a thickened heart; and the church of Laodicea had a complacent spirituality with a hard heart. The heart of each church limited the Holy Spirit's work such that Christ complained that their ekklesia was loveless, was worldly, had wrong doctrine, was dead, or was lukewarm, respectively.

The Holy Spirit has been described in Aramaic as *ruwach* for "spirit" or "wind." When believers are instructed to "be filled with the Spirit" in Ephesians 5:18, the Greek tense is one that indicates that the filling of the Spirit is continuous and not a once-for-all experience.[17] Followers require continuous filling, just as people require oxygen continuously. The Aramaic for "breath" or "spirit" is *ruha*. The Hebrew for "breathe" is *ruach*, and the verb "to breathe" is *linshom*. The breath of life is described first in Genesis for all of God's living creatures.[18] Then King Zedekiah said that the Lord "has given us breath" when he swore his secret oath to the prophet Jeremiah.[19] When speaking about the nation of Israel as bones and tendons in Ezekiel, the Lord says, "I will make breath enter you, and you will come to life."[20]

A fit church invites the breath of the Lord with prayer, obedience, confession, and an attitude of holiness to create worthy believers. Believing and loving causes him to make himself known. The church Body requires the pure life-sustaining fuel of the Holy Spirit for life and optimal functioning. Like individual cells in the human body, believers within the Body of Christ require the Holy Spirit to function. "'Not by might, nor by power, but by my Spirit,' says the Lord Almighty."[21] The Spirit of God can penetrate the spirit of man, and as such penetrates the believing community. Without the presence of the Holy Spirit, the church Body fails and falters. The Holy Spirit serves as a type of gasoline for the spiritual Body's engine.

Running out of gas is a terrible feeling, so much so that most of us will not allow our vehicles to get too low on fuel. Why do Christian leaders allow our churches to "run out" of life's basic sustaining fuel, the Holy Spirit? When churches neglect, ignore, or turn their backs on him, the Holy Spirit is grieved and cannot make himself known. Resisting, doubting, sinning, and refusing to obey him causes the church's engine to spit, sputter, and stop. The Scripture says, "And do not grieve the Holy Spirit of God."[22]

For churches, the heart is the center of spiritual activity and all operations of human life.[23] Some biblical references use "heart" and "soul" interchangeably.[24] Other instances use the heart as the seat of conscience.[25] The heart can be wise,[26] pure,[27] righteous,[28] or even naturally wicked,[29] contaminating one's character and life.[30]

The heart of a church displays the essence of its people. Jesus is the head of the church, and the Holy Spirit is the heart of every church. A church's heart pumps the life-sustaining fuel of the Holy Spirit into its Body. When a church loses the presence of God, it dies. The heartbeat of an ekklesia supplies the sustaining life force that allows for vitality and service. It is important for leadership to encourage the presence of the Holy Spirit during worship, Bible study, and ministry.

The health of an ekklesia is directly proportional to the level of spiritual fitness in its clergy and lay leadership. Fit ekklesias and fit followers will eventually lead to an organic regeneration of the church heart. Spiritually fit leaders are not afflicted with the same sins or fears of their faltering fellows, and they represent excellence within their own faith tribe. Hence the power or *exousia* of Christ flows through them to produce fruitful labor, the spread of the gospel, and the up-building of the church.[31]

True leaders recognize the essential vision of reproducing enthusiasts for Christ within the ekklesia and reaching the next generation by working the heart of Christ into the lives of others in the world. A fit Body exhibits the kind of heart that listens to the will, the way, and the truth of God in the place where each believer or church lives. Faltering churches need a reliable tool to help them change trajectory. Healthy churches need a tool to strengthen and sustain their community's enthusiasm. Hopefully the virtue of Christ's ecclesial DNA will be exposed in established churches and infused into new church plants through a lifestyle of spiritual fitness.

A church with a fit heart develops a fitness lifestyle that results in a deeper, richer experience, "a corporate explosion of spiritual life that displays the Lord Jesus through His every-membered body."[32] Understand that church fitness promotes an organic relationship with Jesus Christ, so believers and assemblies can grow in unity, maturity, and faith. Unless God's clergy and leadership develop a heart of Christ and become fit followers, their churches cannot climb the mountain of change to reach the next generation of believers.

The apostle John, in chapter 15 of his Gospel, says that the Holy Spirit is the Counselor. Jesus explains the holiness of the Holy Spirit in chapter 14, the purpose of the Holy Spirit in chapter 15, and the power of the Holy Spirit in chapter 16. John is trying to explain the key to a spiritual lifestyle: the Holy Spirit.

Without the Holy Spirit, a church becomes a gathering place, merely a space, for people to observe religion while fulfilling a common, self-satisfying purpose. But whenever Jesus is glorified, the Holy Spirit comes![33] Jesus says: "You did not choose me, but I chose you and appointed you to go and bear fruit—fruit that will last—and so that whatever you ask in my name the Father will give you."[34] The Holy Spirit comes to "guide you into all the truth."[35] The empowering presence of the Holy Spirit leads the apostle Paul to say, "I can do all this through him who gives me strength."[36] The breath of the Holy Spirit is essential to the proper functioning of every church.

To be a guest in the Lord's house, the Father's holy sanctuary, the guest must be surrendered as a living sacrifice to the Lord. Such preparation requires the Holy Spirit and is necessary for both the guest and the leadership. The presence of the Holy Spirit makes a church a Holy Sanctuary. The Body of Christ cannot exist without the presence of the Eternal Spirit, Person, and Lordship within the Church.

In a fit church, the Holy Spirit creates a healthy heart that empowers followers to do the will of the Father. A fit Body breathes in the Holy Spirit, which creates a holy sanctuary that will empower, grow, and sustain the believing community.

Ordained Leadership

We already know that Jesus is the head of every church, and the categorical analysis shows that the Mind of Christ is the most important driver for church fitness. Leadership within churches is a major driver contributing to a fit culture. Ordained leadership is central. Pastors, priests, and clergy are the conduit for the Mind of Christ. As called ministers of the faith, they communicate the message from the Head, Jesus, to the members of the Body. In many ways, ordained leadership provides the roadmap for the believer's pilgrimage to experience the life of Christ through the organizational church.

The central nervous system (CNS) of the human body is made up of a network of cells called neurons. These neurons fit together to form nerves. A network of nerves starts in the brain and continues down the spinal cord, exiting the spine at the proper place in order to affect the body. Just as the CNS is the conduit of communication from the thoughts and desires originating from the head, the network of ordained leadership communicates the spiritual information to the Body of Christ.

Preaching is an important message sent down the church's spinal cord or super highway for distribution of God's will to affect every part of the Body. Remember that the style of expository preaching (taken from the categorical analysis) is the specific driver for Body fitness. Expository preaching is the form of preaching that details the meaning of a particular passage of Scripture. How we hear the Word leads us into God's presence so that his transforming power does its divine work as we listen. Communication of the Mind of Christ is stronger when it is coordinated with other corporate acts during worship. Other preaching styles may be important for specific purposes, but if used alone, they may not transmit the Mind of Christ.

Every organ adjusts precisely to the messages sent by the CNS through complicated CNS feedback loops throughout the body. The heart and its accompanying vascular system have some of the most sophisticated feedback mechanisms in the body. As such, the heart and the cardiovascular system (the lay leadership) are in constant communication with the brain through the CNS. Without fit clergy, communication within the Body of Christ is impaired.

God calls ordained clergy and provides them with the necessary spiritual gifts to accomplish their calling. Furthermore, their governing faith tribe commissions them. God communicates spiritually to his unique ministers of the faith, and they should, therefore, communicate that spiritual direction to their believing community. The ordained clergy represent the central nervous system, which communicates the Mind of Christ to the fit Body.

Nerves have an important insulated covering similar to the rubber around an electric cord. This insulating sheath protects and improves the efficiency of nerve communication in the human body. The church staff serves a similar role. They help the clergy carry out their role in an efficient, focused manner. The church staff's role is to equip the Body for service in ministry and mission.[37] The staff serves an important facilitator function. In a fit Body, the church staff is like the supporting structure for the central nervous system of the body.

Vitality is another expression for enthusiasm. It describes a vibrant, fit church. When pastors have lengthy tenures at churches, this positively impacts church vitality. When pastors spend more time on preaching, planning, and leading worship, church vitality also increases.[38] Compensation that the clergy receive has also been positively associated with congregational vitality. Pastors with higher monetary compensation had higher rates of growth.[39] The clergy tend to have strengths and weaknesses, too. Finding complementary co-leadership is helpful in rounding out the needs of each ekklesia.

Although older pastors identify more with the aging church community, younger people are becoming more interested in becoming clergy. Since 2000, millennials have shown increased interest in pursuing careers in ordained ministry. The average age of students enrolling in seminary for a Master in Divinity program is decreasing. At Denver Seminary, the average age has dropped from forty-three in 2000 to thirty-two in 2010. At Duke Divinity School, it dropped to twenty-eight, and at Yale Divinity School, the average incoming age declined to twenty-nine in 2010.[40]

Lay Leadership

The heart of a church is its lay leadership and its members. Leaders are intimately connected to Jesus and serve as a conduit of Christ's love to the Body. Leaders encourage the continuous movement of receiving from God the gift of his presence and giving that gift to others in the church. The Latin origin of the word heart is *cor* and means "cordial" and "courage." In Greek, "heart" is translated *kardia*, from which the medical term *cardia* is derived. In addition to the medical definition, the heart is also known as the center of our personality, especially intuition, feeling, and emotion.[41] In biblical language, the heart is the center of the human spirit from which springs emotion, thought, motivation, courage, and action.[42]

An earthly heart is more than just a functional muscle. It displays the true essence of its owner. For the Christian follower, the heart is the center of his spirit, and it reflects his emotion, thought, motivation, courage, and action. The heart is so important to the body that Solomon said, "Above all else, guard your heart, for everything you do flows from it."[43]

A person cannot embody every gift, trait, or skill necessary to be an effective leader. As such, the industry of leadership development offers books, seminars, and online resources to provide that missing link or secret sauce to help each leader become successful (for a fee, of course). Obtaining leadership skills is helpful, but God provides a different pathway. In the Kingdom, the Holy Spirit provides different spiritual gifts to every Christian. The apostle Paul instructs that the gifts are for use in building up the Church.[44]

As followers join together to form a team, they encompass a more complete complement of the necessary gifts for service. Church followers who help to carry out the Mind of Christ in the church are follower leaders. As such, follower leaders should have no problem partnering with other church leaders. Supporting leaders are sometimes more talented and capable than their acclaimed superiors. During World War II, for example, George Catlett Marshall was the architect of the Marshall Plan, and he rebuilt the U.S. Army in preparation for the war. He served as President Truman's right-hand man. He was the first soldier to win the Nobel Peace Prize in peacetime. "Truman, Eisenhower, and Churchill all said he was the greatest man they had ever known. First-rate co-leaders are a necessity, not a luxury."[45]

The Bible is surfeit of examples of leadership pairs: Aaron and Moses; Mordecai and Esther; Silas and Paul; Barnabas and Mark; Timothy and Paul:, and Jesus and his Apostles. Probably the most important co-leadership team in a fit church is ordained leadership and lay leadership. While the ordained are a conduit for Jesus delivering the Mind of Christ, lay leaders represent a different pathway that is interrelated to the heart of their church, the cardiovascular system.

Just as an athlete must take care of his or her body, so should a church take care of its structures and its believing community. Christian behavior and the unity of the Body are a function of the Head, Holy Spirit, and leadership. Looking back at the bride metaphor, there is a precedent for the Church as bride to care for herself. Clinically, much of that care comes from the ordained and lay leadership among the community of believers. The spiritual gifts of leadership[46] and administration[47] are given to some believers. These individuals should have the authority to administer the affairs of the church and care for the church's staff.

Negligence in maintaining the affairs of the church can be more detrimental than neglecting any vehicle. Maintenance of the church requires time in the "repair shop." Beyond poor performance, disrepair, or sunk cost while in the shop for repair, a foothold for sin and for quenching the Holy Spirit may result. The time, labor, and expense to properly manage church affairs are essential to the health of the Body of Christ, the believing community. Leadership in each church uses different techniques and organizational philosophy for administration and management within their church. The staff must understand the Mind of Christ for their church, and the pastor is essential to helping keep the staff on track. Lay leadership controls conflict, manages discipline, and regulates Christian behavior within the church.

That conflict arises when people work together is a fact. Even the New Testament ekklesias described in Acts 6 were trying to manage the increasing number of believers along with their concerns and complaints. Sides were being drawn between the Grecian Jews and the Hebraic Jews over the importance of preserving Jewish custom. The solution was the selection of leaders, "seven men from among you who are known to be full of the Spirit and wisdom. We will turn this responsibility over to them."[48] Thus the leader Stephen was introduced; he and the others were chosen to help solve the conflict.

Notice the result of leadership. First, "This proposal pleased the whole group."[49] Then, "So the word of God spread. The number of disciples in Jerusalem increased rapidly, and a large number of priests became obedient to the faith."[50]

The roles of deacons[51] and elders[52] or their equivalent are carefully revealed in the Bible. Authors like Henry and Richard Blackaby in their book *Spiritual Leadership: Moving People on to God's Agenda* and Mark Dever in his book *9 Marks of a Healthy Church* also reveal the important function of leadership to churches. "The Christian leader of the future is the one who truly knows the heart of God as it has become flesh, 'a heart of flesh', in Jesus."[53] When decisions are made using the heart of Christ, the ekklesia guarantees the fulfillment of its mission and the true direction of its vision. The heart of a fit church is represented by the lay leadership who express the presence of God and the love of Christ to the Body.

Fit Followers

There are over 650 muscles in the human body.[54] Some are smooth like those in the blood vessels, and some are striated like those in our arms and legs. In this fitness model, the Body of Christ has many members or parts that are all connected and interconnected.[55] Every muscle is part of a muscle group that has specific abilities and can perform specific tasks. Sometimes these muscle groups work in unison to accomplish complex movements.

For example, the hand has seventeen muscles that affect the movements of the fingers, thumb, and hand. First the mind must decide what task it wants to perform. Then it wills and directs the action to occur. Based upon sensorimotor feedback mechanisms, the hand carries out the action expertly without additional thought or delay. The Body of Christ can work just as efficiently.

The members of the Body, followers, work the same way as muscles. Groups of believers work together in concert to carry out tasks ordained by the leadership. "Just as a body, though one, has many parts, but all its many parts form one body."[56] The compilation of spiritual gifts within a group provides guidance and certain gifts for ministry and shepherding to be accomplished within community. Faithful enthusiastic believers are comparable to robust strong muscles by which "all things" can be accomplished.[57]

When the Body maintains the proper diet and exercise regimen, its members will be healthy. A Body that practices spiritual disciplines and trains in the fitness center will grow strong, faithful muscles: faith fitness. Members are meant to work out in community, not alone. For some, the purpose of personal fitness is egocentric—to become a physical specimen or fitness "peacock." Believers who work out their salvation alone and then strut around the churchyard showing off are displaying a poor version of Christianity, one that focuses on the self, not Christ.

Followers must be robust in the Lord. The apostle Paul says, "I urge you to live a life worthy of the calling you have received."[58] Christian living should be characterized by newness of life,[59] good works,[60] love,[61] wisdom,[62] truth,[63] and obedience.[64] A fit Body attempts to create worthy followers. Fitness is worthiness. The Greek word for "worthy" is *axios*. "It declares the perfect congruity between the life on earth and the issue and reward of the life in heaven. And it holds up to us the great principle that purity here is crowned with glory hereafter."[65]

The Bible holds many descriptors for the worthy believer. Each adds to the portrait of a fit follower. They must be pure[66] and live a holy life.[67] They do not put out the Spirit's fire.[68] A follower is like a good soldier who fights the good fight[69] and endures hardships.[70] Other descriptors include an athlete,[71] son,[72] worker,[73] student,[74] vessel and servant.[75] Jesus said of the church at Sardis, "Yet you have a few people in Sardis who have not soiled their clothes. They will walk with me, dressed in white, for they are worthy."[76] Jesus demonstrates that believers should still strive to be worthy followers, even if they are in a faltering church. Building up worthy followers is the by-product of a fit church.

In Len Sweet's book *I Am a Follower,* a video displays a random fellow dancing at a festival. A brave and courageous first follower steps in to join the dance. "When we dance along with Jesus, we become disciples within his incarnated body and baptized in the Spirit with the grace of his resurrection life."[77] About first followers Sweet says, "They are not afraid to stand up and dance to a different beat."[78] You, the reader, may be a first follower looking to improve the health of your ekklesia. Followers, like muscles, thrive when they are stretched to capacity solely dedicated to the purpose God intended. Followers want to join the Lord of the dance.

Evangelism

We are discussing the major drivers of church fitness, and evangelism is one of them. U.S. churches haven't kept pace with population growth. From 1990 to 2006, the nation's population increased by a net 51.8 million people, to about 300 million. During that time, more than 91 million new people have been born in the United States (and 39.6 million have died), but total church attendance did not change at all, with 52 million attending worship on any given Sunday. The percentage of Americans who attended worship on any given weekend declined from 20.4 percent in 1990 to 17.5 percent in 2005.

In the 1800s, there were between 200 and 400 new churches per 1 million people, but that decreased by half, to between 100 and 200, during the 1900s. During this new millennium, new churches are at 100 per 1 million people. Just to keep up with population growth, over 7,200 churches of any Christian sect would need to be started each year; believing communities must birth a new church at a rate better than one birth for every 100 established churches. At present, about half those numbers of churches are started. Christian sects that are planting less than one church for every 100 established churches are declining the fastest.[79] U.S. churches have not been keeping up with population growth. This underscores the importance of *Faith Fitness*. The real question is: *Why* haven't U.S. churches kept pace with population growth? Christianity is exploding in almost every continent except Europe and North America. People are excited to know the person of Jesus Christ, and many new church starts are occurring.

For churches in Europe and North America, a different social and religious construct has created a new moraine, which has left church leaders confused, out of touch, and mostly irrelevant to the burgeoning unbelieving population. It is fair to say that we have passed the hump of transition, since we are now left with a new, altered landscape. We can argue about the timing, the contributing factors, or the response to postmodernism, but to deny its impact on the marketplace of unbelievers is foolhardy.

The real consequence of this post-Christian world on the church is that many leaders have turned inward, to a shrinking universe of adherents ready to defend their selfish wants, instead of turning outward, to build in and to plant in the life of others.[80] The end result is the lack of a proper vision, purpose, and focus. Though we are used to harvesting that which we have not sown, we must learn to cultivate, plant, and fertilize before we can hope to reach unbelievers. The Body is neither unified nor knowledgeable enough to implement a proper strategy to share the gospel and address the needs of the least, the lost, and the needy of this post-Christian world.

The average annual growth rate for a new church is 12 percent. The growth rate declines to 4 percent by year ten. The growth rate decreases to 1 percent by year twenty and is stable for the next twenty to twenty-five years, much like in people. The growth rate is consistent with the natural history of aging. Senescence, the body's decline with aging, begins in the forties and continues until the end; however, some churches survive for two hundred years. The oldest churches survive because they refresh themselves with enthusiasts and they reinvent their purpose.[81]

The American Church Research Project has created a benchmark to demonstrate what a "healthy denomination" attendance looks like. In their profile, 16 percent of a denomination's attendance comes from new churches, 36 percent of their attendance comes from churches eleven to forty years old, and 48 percent of their attendance comes from churches over forty years of age. The distribution for mainline denominational families is closer to 2 percent attendance from new churches and over 80 percent from churches over forty years old![82]

Annual Percent Growth Trend

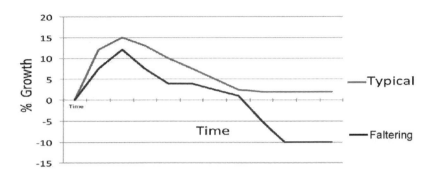

Over time, churches age like people do (see the "Typical" church curve in the graph above). Denominations are declining at an alarming rate (see the "Faltering" church curve in graph). Notice that growth remains positive in the Typical church. Faltering churches have member losses and negative growth. The church aging cycle is an important aspect of wellness. New churches are usually birthed in high population growth areas.[83] Many times the age of a community's churches corresponds to that region's population growth. Like a newborn, the fastest growth is in the early years.

How aging churches decline is unique to the path their leadership follows. Aging has other interesting effects on the Body. As churches age, members enjoy an increased income and socioeconomic status. The proportion of female to male members increases with age. The abundance or prevalence of children and youth declines with age. Attendance at church functions, including Bible studies, declines with aging members, and the population of members becomes more racially homogenous. (In American mainline churches, this often means they become more white.) All these changes in aging have a negative effect on growth, enthusiasm, and vitality.

The maternal desire to reproduce offspring is one of the most powerful forces on earth. The condition of infertility, though, weighs heavily on those women and men who fail to conceive and reproduce. Churches have an ecclesial programming to reproduce, too. Churches may be limited by institutional infertility, disease, or the absence of the Holy Spirit. Becoming a healthy and fit ekklesia allows them to fulfill the vision of the Lord to pass the Kingdom's ecclesial genes to the next generation of believers. The previous definition of fitness, "the capacity to survive and transmit one's genotype to reproductively fertile offspring," is relevant for both humans and the Church.

One of the most powerful drivers of church fitness is evangelism: building up the next generation of believers. It tied for second in the categorical analysis (behind the Mind of Christ—vision, purpose, mission, behavior). Evangelism is why the Body runs the race. It is the essence of church survival. Without churches reaching Haywood's reproductive threshold, extinction is plausible, and irrelevance is likely within the Kingdom.

We've already seen in fit New Testament churches (in Smyrna, Philadelphia, and Thessalonica) that being succession-minded and being focused on soul winning were important. The mission of these ekklesias was exemplified in the Body metaphor: "Love your neighbor as yourself,"[84] and, "Go and make disciples of all nations."[85] In too many churches, evangelism and new church starts have little priority. Thus, many denominations' birth rates are not keeping up with their death rates. But for the fit church, Kingdom building is the *raison d'être*!

On average, one American church closes its doors permanently and dies every thirty-five minutes of the day. Between 2000 and 2005, over 3,700 churches closed. The majority died of old age or diseases like lack of faith. Denominations sell the properties to help their districts generate revenue for other church projects. Churches are purchased to become family homes or small businesses. Some churches are renovated to become bars or strip clubs—a terrible tribute to a building of spiritual legacy where so many lives were saved, memories made, and generations impacted. Even secular city councils, in some cases, have passed ordinances to prevent these old historic buildings with their elegant stained glass and steeples from falling prey to such egregious use.[86,87]

Infant mortality is a problem, too. Ten to 50 percent of church deaths are from newly birthed churches that don't survive the initial period; therefore, some of the fastest growing sects of Christianity are among those with the highest rate of church mortality! Some denominations have a falsely low death rate that is lower than average for two reasons. First, there were very few births, therefore they have a low infant mortality. Second, the denomination created assisted living "charges," clusters of small frail churches serviced by a pastor circuit that kept churches alive longer.[88]

Aging is inevitable. The most important disposition is to age well or to finish well in life. Healthy aging is as important for believing communities as it is for its clergy and its members. Do you know the antidote for aging and congregational death? One of the most important accomplishments of any church is starting new churches. It is the ultimate sign of church fitness. It can only be achieved with faith fitness.

New church births are too low in almost every denomination, but especially in mainline sects. My own faith tribe is not performing very well, with a planting rate of only 0.2 percent. A birth rate of 2 percent is necessary to keep up with population growth. That's tenfold the number of church starts needed. The average birth rate among the thirteen largest denominations is still only 1.6 percent. A birth rate of 0.2 percent (one church for every 500 established churches) is not only far below the average, but it is the lowest planting rate among the thirteen largest denominations.

Reaching a critical mass of seventy people in attendance by the end of the first year is key for the survival of any new church plant. To be effective at reproduction, a denomination must grow newly birthed churches with a growth rate above 10 percent per year during the first seven years. Strong support from the parent church during the critical early years is essential for new plant survival.[89]

More research is needed on church starts and planting. The Bible demonstrates four basic planting styles that have been discussed in detail elsewhere.[90] Today, parent churches use hybrids of these models to birth new believing communities. Some of the more common examples follow, along with a corresponding reference for more study.

1 The seed or Antioch model

The parent church sends a planter or apostle to plant a new church away from the parent church. The planter returns intermittently to the parent church to resupply and then returns to the field to start new churches. Examples of the apostle Paul and his missionaries planting churches in Galatia, Greece, and Asia Minor can be found in Acts 14-16.

2 The seedling or Jerusalem model

The parent church starts a church within its own congregation for the purpose of transplanting the people to another locality to continue the new church. An example is the Jerusalem church found in Acts 2:14-8:3.

3 The planter or Ephesian model

The parent church trains and commissions apostles for church starts. These planters leave the parent church with some resources to start a new church where the planter stays and grows the new church. An example is the Ephesian church in Acts 19, where Paul trained eight men at the Hall of Tyrannus before sending them over to Asia Minor to plant churches.

4 The cutting or Roman model

The parent church transplants small groups of its members to specific mission locations to grow a new arm of the original church. Organizational leadership, structure and roles were established prior to the move. An example is Priscilla and Aquila in Rome, found in Acts chapter 18.

5 The multisite "satellite" model

This model could be a derivative of the Roman model above. The parent church opens an extension of their church at a new, underserved site in hopes of growing the church in niches along generational or ministry lines.[91] This technique is very popular today among large, successful churches that understand the concept of scaling an organization. The downside of the satellite model is increased overall cost, high marginal cost for each new member, and more difficult management of free-riders.

The ten largest churches in the U.S. have forty-one satellite churches among them. The availability of inexpensive retail property and high-tech video links has accelerated the use of multisite churches. Strategies for niche ministry have enabled the model to attract nonbelievers so that a relationship with God, not the culture of the church, is stressed. Not all members of the denominational family have embraced the multisite model, though. Some miss the closer ties with their pastor and debate the pros and cons of using video links in place of additional pastors. The multisite strategy tends to be an outreach of independent churches and those focused on evangelism.[92]

In striving for a fit culture, leaders can use the correlation of the human body with the Body of Christ and use the drivers of church health to create a fit church. Lay leaders are essential co-leaders with ordained clergy to fulfill the vision, mission, and purpose of their churches.

One bread, one body, one Lord of all,
One cup of blessing which we bless.
We, though many throughout the earth,
We are one body in this one Lord.
John B. Foley

Fitness Moment

- The functioning of the church organization has many parallels to the human body.
- Christ is the head, ordained clergy is the central nervous system, and lay leadership is the cardiovascular system.
- The Holy Spirit gives every ekklesia its heartbeat and life.
- Leadership must be fit to lead. They should create the vision, purpose, and mission of the church and faithfully build a culture that lives it out.
- The role of ordained leadership is to transmit the mind of Christ to the Body.
- Non-ordained leadership should serve as co-leaders with ordained clergy.
- Evangelism is a major driver of church health that leads to a fit church culture.
- As church leaders armed with the information in *Faith Fitness*, it is time to respond, as the next prescription directs.

Respond

Sig: *follow the instructions*
Refill(s): *prn — as needed*
Comments: *No substitutions permitted*

Whoever serves me must follow me;
and where I am, my servant also will be.
My Father will honor the one who serves me.[93]

Coepit facere is Latin for "begin to act." Go. Do. Jesus wants us to follow him now. Immediacy is important to him. He wants our churches to commit and to respond to him. Refurbishment and organizational changes may be necessary, but for now, just get started. Our ekklesias have a special purpose in the Kingdom, despite our limitations.

God uses the morbidity of man to accomplish his purpose. There are many stories of God stripping away any semblance of human power to demonstrate his glory. If you want to see a Who's Who of Bible characters, see the "Hall of Faith" in the eleventh chapter of Hebrews. In every case, the mature faith of the ordinary follower was used by God to accomplish his supernatural purpose in building his Kingdom.

Heroes of the faith develop in every generation in nearly every locality. Some are known, but most are not. These fit followers hone their spiritual muscles through intimate prayer, reading the Word, and faithfully doing God's will. For spiritual heroes of the faith, ministry and mission are not done alone. They are done on the field of life with many spectators and witnesses. This vision creates a spiritual image of an athletic contest where the spiritual giants of the past are cheering us on through prayerful inspiration and faithful encouragement to help us persevere in the long race. "As long as it is day, we must do the works of him who sent me."[94] Our work is touching others in their life where we are using our God-given gifts.

By witnessing God's supernatural power in mission, the Body learns how to apply the principles from the Word of God, how prayer builds faith, and how the Body grows through obedience and holiness. Doing the mission of the Church with community perfects the faith of its followers. It teaches that the consequences of obedience can be left with him.

Do you want to summit the fitness spectrum? This book started by introducing us to an elite climber who listened to the mountain to learn how to climb the most difficult test of his lifetime. As a leader in your church, you have a difficult task, but by listening to and accessing the power of Jesus Christ, you can participate in this faith fitness journey.

Decide to climb the fitness spectrum individually and as a leadership team. Choose to climb the difficult moraine of change that is necessary for your church to be relevant again. You've had an opportunity to understand the importance of church fitness, to transform your heart with the series of prescriptions, and to meet with other leaders from your church to complete the fitness exercises.

By adopting and living the ingredients of a healthy church, by committing leadership to participate in this faith fitness movement, and by organizationally creating the spiritual fitness site concept, you have responded to the challenge of becoming a wellness-oriented church. Your next step is to create excitement within your ekklesia by developing the Mind of Christ, creating a new vision, purpose, and mission. Now followers within your ekklesia have a direction and a goal to work toward. Decide on the generation of people within your measure of rule that you want to draw to your church. Develop a strategy by using the wellness toolbox. When leadership selects useful drivers from the wellness toolbox, a languid church can transform to a wellness-oriented church that is bringing in new members and building up fit followers. Leaders who are already part of a wellness-oriented church should make the final push to become a fit church. Strive to create fit followers who build up and plant new churches within the Kingdom. By reaching the summit, the fit ekklesia is focused outward on multiplying the Kingdom, despite its limitations.

You can be a leader who follows Christ, leads other believers, and reaches the lost. The view from the top is a fit church culture and faith fitness.

6

FITNESS LIFESTYLE

*As for other matters, brothers and sisters, we instructed you how to live
in order to please God, as in fact you are living.
Now we ask you and urge you in the Lord
Jesus to do this more and more.*
1 Thessalonians 4:1

For me, the Olympic games encompass the ultimate expression of physical fitness. I really enjoyed watching the most recent Olympics, especially Rio de Janeiro 2016, Sochi 2014, and London 2012. The best of the best athletes from around the world competed for the ultimate sports prize: an Olympic Medal. People gathered from around the world to watch these competitions. As a little boy, I remember following the daily medal count to see how the United States compared to other countries.

The apostle Paul was fond of depicting a believer as an athlete in a game[1] or as a prizefighter.[2] He viewed believers as elite spiritual athletes. Both must live a fitness lifestyle in order to perform optimally. Proper dietary regimens, training routines, and the sacrifice of unhealthy habits are all necessary. The fitness lifestyle allows the believer to follow Paul's instruction, "let us run with perseverance the race marked out for us."[3] Participating in the Lord's race is never done in solitude, for we are being watched by "a great crowd of witnesses."

Church leadership is about creating the culture and resources so that unbelievers come to know the gospel of Christ and then develop into fit followers. To be successful, churches must develop a fit Body, too. Churches with the highest level of spiritual fitness empower their worthy followers to love others, share the gospel, and multiply the Kingdom. Now that leaders have had an opportunity to incorporate the healthy ingredients and fit archetype into their culture, develop the Mind of Christ for their ekklesia, use the wellness toolbox to build a strategy to accomplish their new mission, and create a fit Body for communication, leaders can focus on believer development and the fitness lifestyle. This chapter demonstrates a church culture that lives in order to please God.

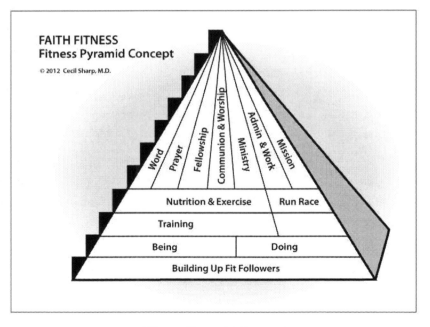

Fitness Pyramid Concept

Fitness Habits

When I was in primary school, my teachers would use the food pyramid to help explain the relationships between the different food groups. The Faith Fitness Pyramid demonstrates the habits for maturing and assimilating members into committed followers, especially new converts. It does so by optimizing every member's fitness level so they become enthusiasts, fully participating in the life of their community. The pyramid exposes the benefits of building up the Body through organizational fitness and member fitness.

The Faith Fitness Pyramid requires the presence of the Holy Spirit. Becoming fit depends on coming into a deeper relationship and understanding of Christ. The Fitness Pyramid is a visual depiction of the remaining church fitness drivers. It shows that spiritual nutrition involves Scripture, prayer, fellowship, and holy communion. Ministry, which includes shepherding, discipleship, and pastoral care, represents types of in-house spiritual exercises. Churches that use proper nutrition and exercises in a regimen of training teach believers to *be* followers. After these followers hone their training in the safety of a community of other loving followers, they enter the world to run the race and *do* as fit followers.

The following table, Fitness Habits, lists the remainder of the Fitness Drivers (taken from the categorical analysis of ordained leaders) along with their church body corollary. The comparison is not meant to limit the elements of the gospel that we've determined to be important to fitness in the Body of Christ. The comparison draws analogies from general principles of health and fits into the concept of spiritual fitness so church leaders have a point of reference when training their constituents and followers. The church fitness drivers from Fitness Habits complement the drivers from the Fit Body and together complete the most important church health drivers. Remember that more than 50 percent of theologians whose work we examined stated that the health of the church was affected by the Mind of Christ (vision, purpose, unity, and Christian behavior), evangelism, leadership, discipleship, worship, and the Holy Spirit. Fellowship,

Scripture, prayer, structures, preaching, finance, and staff were important church drivers for less than 50 percent of the theologians.

Fitness Driver	Conditioning Corollary
The Spiritual Disciplines	Dietary fuel
Scripture	Bread of life
Prayer	Growth
Fellowship	Fulfillment
Holy Communion	Essential vitamin of the Church
Worship	Corporate immersion
Discipleship	T^5 Training – Being (Christian maturity, equipping, and discipline)
Shepherding	T^5 Training – Being (focus on member pastoral care and programs)
Service	T^5 Training – Doing, Run the Race (ministry among believers and mission among non-believers)

Fitness Habits

The Spiritual Disciplines

Fuel for the human body is made up of three basic ingredients: sugar (carbohydrate), protein, and fat. Nutritionists tell us that our intake of these fuels should be balanced: about 60-65 percent carbohydrate, 15-20 percent protein, and 25-30 percent fat. Nearly every food that is ingested contains varying amounts of each. Specific food groups are therefore recommended for our daily intake to maintain a healthy diet. One of the biggest problems in U.S. healthcare today is obesity caused by unhealthy eating habits and lack of exercise. The end result becomes lost productivity, disease, generational illness, and escalating costs. Excess of processed food, sugars, and artificial sweeteners have become the norm in the average American diet.

The Body of Christ also requires a balanced diet. The Word of God provides the template for the Body's fuel. Jewish law commanded annual attendance at the three feasts in Jerusalem by adult males and their families. When Jesus was twelve years old, the family's annual pilgrimage at the Feast of Passover took a remarkable twist. Mary and Joseph demonstrated their ordinary parenting skills during their return home when they noticed that Jesus was not with them; he was left behind in Jerusalem! After searching for him for three days, they found him in the temple courts. At twelve years old, Jewish boys were learning how to participate in the religious community. Why didn't Mary look in the temple first? After all, God spoke to her through his angel about her immaculate conception. I think Mary woke up to Jesus's manhood and purpose when he answered her questions about where he'd been while she had been anxiously searching for him: "Why were you searching for me? Didn't you know I had to be in my Father house?"[4]

What did Jesus do in the temple? What was his Father's business? Jesus gathered among other Jews and rabbis, learned about Scripture by listening and asking questions, and taught about God while everyone who heard him was amazed at his understanding and his answers.[5] "'My food,' said Jesus, 'is to do the will of him who sent me and to finish his work.'"[6] God provided the fuel and passion for Jesus to learn and teach others about him.

In Acts 2:42, Luke describes the spiritual food of the disciples: "They devoted themselves to the apostles' teaching and to fellowship, to the breaking of bread and to prayer." Fuel for the spiritual body and the Body of Christ also has four main ingredients: Scripture, fellowship, holy communion, and prayer. A lack of any of these ingredients leaves the Body afflicted with not only a shameful lifestyle that contributes to the unfit Body but also a poor witness of the gospel. This spiritual food awakens the soul of followers to the joy of his presence! These spiritual habits create an efficient, enjoyable connection to Christ. Absence of this fuel lulls the soul into a sedentary or even comatose condition.

Every cell and tissue of the human body must maintain or grow depending on its function. The necessary fuel for that maintenance and growth is sugar, protein, and fat. As always, balance of these constituents is the key. The important take-home message for the fit church or fit believer is that the balance of these spiritual fuels maintains the Body.

In *Faith Fitness*, the basic spiritual food groups for churches are Scripture, fellowship, holy communion, and prayer. Let's take a look at each of these dietary ingredients.

Scripture

Refined sugar is a pure carbohydrate. Fruits also contain sugar and fiber. Vegetables contain more complex sugars, called carbohydrates, as well as fiber. Carbohydrates are ingested, broken down, and metabolized to become the basic building block for cell energy, a sugar called glucose. During pregnancy, one of the placenta's main roles is to supply glucose to the fetus; a constant and steady flow of glucose perfectly grows and develops the tender baby. Glucose is also the basic nutrient for the brain. Most patients that are admitted to the hospital receive a life-sustaining intravenous fluid solution containing glucose and water.

Sugar/carbohydrates are a key component of bread, one of the metaphors Jesus frequently uses to describe how the Word of God nourishes us spiritually.[7] Scripture is like sugar, and carbohydrates more generally, to the human body. The Word of God is the basic fuel for every believer and for the Church, just as the sugar glucose is the cellular building block for the body. The Word of God penetrates deep within the body, too. It "penetrates even to dividing soul and spirit, joints and marrow; it judges the thoughts and attitudes of the heart."[8]

Scripture is like the body's fundamental nutritional requirement: sugar. Taken in excess over a period of time, sugar can cause an aging body to become insulin resistant, which can lead to diabetes, a serious, debilitating condition affecting the body's function. When a church Body ingests Scripture predominantly at the expense of the other fuels, the Body becomes imbalanced with the disease of a judgmental heart that lacks the love of Christ. Like insulin, only repentance and the mercy of God can control this affliction. Balanced nutrition and exercise may reverse it completely.

Fellowship

Oils like safflower, olive, or peanut all contain fat. Vegetables contain healthier oils than the oils found in animal fat, which are highly saturated and more difficult for the body to process. Fat has the highest calorie count per unit of weight, nine calories per gram, as compared to protein or sugar, which have about 3.5 calories per gram. Excess intake of most any nutrient is converted in the body to fat and stored in adipose cells. The basic element of fat is a fatty acid. Certain fatty acids cannot be manufactured in the human body (linoleic and linolenic fatty acids) and are therefore "essential" for growth.

Fellowship is like another of the body's fundamental nutritional requirements, fat. The fellowship of believers is one of the most enjoyable and stimulating associations in the believing community. The apostles treasured their time in fellowship with Jesus. Peter, James, and John were known as the inner circle of Jesus's friends. Fellowship is an important ingredient in worship,[9] prayer,[10] education,[11] discipleship, shepherding, and serving.[12] Fellowship meets an important relational need and models followership. Today's Millennials are horizontally programmed; they are deeply connected in fellowship to their like-minded community.

In *Faith Fitness*, the fellowship of believers represents the fat of spiritual food. The habit of taking in excess fat encourages fat storage, which yields an overweight, sedentary, and unhealthy body. An overweight Body only craves more fellowship, not the love of Christ. In addition, fellowship without the other fuels clogs the channels of communication (blood vessels) within the Body, which disrupts the functioning of the lay and ordained leadership (cardiovascular and central nervous systems).

In *Faith Fitness*, the basic spiritual food groups for churches are Scripture, fellowship, and prayer. An organization that intentionally teaches believers proper spiritual nutritional habits is poised to reproduce fit followers.

Holy Communion

Think about what the absence of just one vitamin does to the body. Sailors long ago learned the consequences of vitamin C deficiency on long voyages; it caused scurvy and infection. The absence of vitamin D leaves bones brittle and broken. Vitamin A deficiency gives night blindness and increases the risk of infection. B12 deficiency leaves the body with weight loss and anemia. You get the picture. A body without essential vitamins becomes diseased and dies. Now imagine what would happen if a human body was deficient in all of those vitamins.

Jesus's last supper is described in Luke 22, first as a sharing of the bread and the cup, and second as a reminder of God's love and grace as demonstrated by the sacrifice of his Son. The bread is given in remembrance of Jesus's substitutionary sacrifice on the cross, and, "This cup is the new covenant in my blood, which is poured out for you."[13] Just as the bread is given in remembrance of the body of Christ broken for believers, the wine (or juice) is given in remembrance of the blood of Christ shed for believers. This holy sacrament or meal is as vital to the individual believer as to the Church as a whole. Communion has an essential role within the worship service; it defines who we are as followers. It takes us back to the cross, where we remember that we were slaves to sin and death; and it takes us ahead, where we will commune with him in the Kingdom of heaven. Holy communion is like a multivitamin for the body: the only source of vitamins for the soul of the body.

In *Faith Fitness*, holy communion is the essential ingredient required for the Body to function. Though the frequency of participation varies in the different faith tribes, this sacrament reinforces the Bride, the Branch, and the Body metaphors used throughout the New Testament. Failing to understand and to remember Jesus's sacrifice removes the Christ from Christians and leaves the Church as a faltered archetype!

Prayer

Nuts and legumes are an important source of protein. Other sources of protein are fish, eggs, cheese, and meat. Protein is the key ingredient for cellular and tissue growth. Cells grow in two ways. The growth of a tissue by an increase in cell numbers is called "mitosis," and the growth of a tissue by cell size is called "meiosis." During the body's development and maturation in the childhood years, growth occurs mainly by cell mitosis. A baby is able to double his birth weight within three months because of the increase in cell numbers. Every tissue in the body has its own timeline for cell growth.

Muscles and skin are examples of tissues that have ongoing needs for growth. Body builders can build muscle by ingesting large amounts of protein and working their muscles hard. During pregnancy, a woman's tissues and cells grow in size to accommodate the increasing needs of the growing baby. Protein is an essential building block of all growth.

Prayer is like the body's fundamental nutritional requirement, protein. Jesus taught his disciples much about prayer. He demonstrated how to pray,[14] how prayer relates to believing and receiving,[15] and how powerful prayer is.[16] Prayer was Jesus's main source of intimacy with his Father; it remains the main source for all of us today. The book of Acts describes the importance of prayer to that first ekklesia of believers, "They all joined together constantly in prayer."[17] Prayer is the protein of spiritual food. It is the essential ingredient for personal discipleship, for maturing church staff, and for growing ministry.

For most believers, prayer time is divided into contemplation, meditation, and intercession, but the conventional acronym "A.C.T.S." is recognized as a recipe for prayer: adoration, confession,[18] thanksgiving, and supplication (or intercession).[19] Another tool sometimes employed with prayer is fasting.[20]

The spiritual discipline of prayer is the protein that builds faith among the Body. A Body cannot grow without prayer, but too much protein leaves the Body puffed up, arrogant, and more focused on self than community. An excess of protein without sugar or fat poisons the body with the by-products of an inactive, loveless metabolism. The members (muscles) are made for performing the work and will of the Lord through the community.

Worship

Water plays a central role in the Bible. In the creation story in Genesis, "The Spirit of God was hovering over the waters."[21] Jesus's baptism in the Jordan River seems to recall this verse; the Holy Spirit descended on Jesus after he came up out of the water.[22] With the authority of God, Jesus commanded his disciples to go and baptize in the name of the Father.

The Bible is surfeit with metaphors of water. Jesus says, "If anyone is thirsty, let him come to me and drink. Whoever believes in Me, as the Scripture has said: 'Streams of living water will flow from within him.'"[23] In the Bible, water and the blood of Christ are as inseparable as the water molecules hydrogen and oxygen, H_2O. From Jesus's first miracle at the wedding of Canaan when he turned water into wine, to his miracle on the cross when his side was pierced, water had a central place in his ministry.

The Bible uses this metaphor to emphasize the idea that the worship of God is the key to corporate spiritual life. Worship is a central focus of the Church. Worship takes place both formally in a corporate setting and informally within the heart of believers. It is as essential to the health of any church as water is to the human body. Biologic life begins with the body submerged in amniotic fluid, and the life of any believing community begins in Christ with worship. Just as the human body is made up of mostly water, the fit Body is filled with worship to our Lord and Savior.

Have you ever craved water? Thirst is a miserable feeling created by your body physiologically responding to its need for an adequate supply. Every person requires eight glasses per day for hydration. Though this may seem simple, many people don't get enough water. For example, the most common cause of emergency room visits among the elderly is dehydration. Jesus was thirsty when he asked the Samaritan woman for a drink at Jacob's well. But as essential as water is to physical survival, it is not enough. Jesus points to an even greater need when he tells her: "If you knew the gift of God and who it is that asks you for a drink, you would have asked him and he would have given you living water… whoever drinks the water I give them will never thirst. Indeed, the water I give them will become in them a spring of water welling up to eternal life."[24]

The spiritual Body thirsts for Christ. It can only be quenched by the spiritual worship of our Lord God. In the absence of true worship, the Body becomes spiritually dehydrated and functionally afflicted. Jesus quoted Isaiah, saying, "These people honor me with their lips, but their hearts are far from me. They worship me in vain."[25]

In *Faith Fitness* the ubiquitous, hydrating, refreshing, and cleansing functions of water represent the importance of worship for the Body in training and service.

Discipleship, Shepherding, and Service

Historically, the Church has been a significant wellspring where people come to know Jesus Christ, are trained to become mature disciples, and become heroes of the faith. But in order to run the race marked out for us, we must first train and get into shape. Training requires the proper diet, training habits, and exercise. By leaving ineffectual pursuits, useless trifles, and sin behind, believers can focus on following Christ.

Churches represent the foundational training center where believers of all fitness levels develop into optimally fit spiritual athletes. The ability to train in clean, healthy air with other athletes, to stay hydrated, and to take in a balanced diet creates a "no excuses" environment for development. All great athletes spend hours in practice for every minute of competition. Just as exercise is important to produce cardiovascular health, endurance, confidence, and mental toughness, so reaching our neighbors in the world is that unique fruit that exhibits the love of Christ.

By exercising the muscles in a disciplined manner, an athlete builds the physical, mental, and physiologic toughness to compete at an elite level. Remember the natural history of converts that we discussed earlier in the chapter "Understanding Fitness": new believers enter an enthusiastic period after their conversion. From this point forward, new Christians should be brought up in the faith. Maturation of believers begins with newborn believers and progresses to the spiritually mature adult. Spiritual maturity is tied to faith, not to age. Ministry, discipleship, and shepherding within community exercise and train the community's spiritual muscles.

Discipleship and shepherding can be two sides of the same coin. Discipleship involves the journey of spiritual maturity, and shepherding is a type of maturity involving the care of church members. Ken Hemphill's book *The Antioch Effect*[26] describes the stages of believer maturation and provides insight and structure for accomplishing this training in the believing community. Ultimately, the ekklesia wants to produce a set of robust believers who are accomplished in evangelism and reproductive ministry.

Paul demonstrates the purpose in discipling the believer by instructing Timothy to reproduce himself by equipping faithful servants who would teach others.[27] Evangelism produces new believers, but discipleship reproduces fully committed, enthusiastic members.

Hemphill says, "The goal of every believer should not only be involvement in ministry, but also training others to be ministers."[28] Mature followers lead others into fitness by sharing, teaching, and doing together. Does your church have a program for discipling and maturing new converts and new members? How about established members? Since most churches have few new converts, a formal system of discipleship may not exist. Could this factor be a major contributor to the decreasing number of offspring returning to churches?

The community needs to care for one another and meet each other's needs through shepherding. Psalm 23 demonstrates Jesus's role as shepherd. In John 10, he speaks about the shepherd and the flock. He says, "I am the gate for the sheep," and, "I am the good shepherd."[29]

Following his example, we are all to care for one another, especially in sickness and in sin. In Acts 20:28 the early ekklesia was instructed to, "Keep watch over yourselves and all the flock of which the Holy Spirit has made you overseers. Be shepherds of the church of God." A defining moment for Peter was when Jesus asked him three times, "Simon son of John, do you love me?" To emphasize an important point to Peter, Jesus instructed Peter to, "Feed my sheep," and "Take care of my sheep."[30]

The believing community will have needs, and shepherding its people is a necessary part of loving your brothers and sisters in Christ. It is easy to love someone who loves us back. Shepherding members of the flock represents a good, but sometimes challenging, training ground because the mission field involves loving others who may not love us back. In fact, both discipling and shepherding allow us to practice our "loving skills" in the church where members may be more forgiving of mistakes.

By training daily among other believers, we can improve our skills so that when we enter the race, we're more equipped to do God's will. Ministry including discipleship, shepherding, and pastoral care serves as an in-house training ground that transforms and reproduces believers into worthy, fit followers. The habits of a body in training are very important in body building, reproducing, or building up fit followers. The Fitness Pyramid provides a picture of the necessary habits of a church where leadership is taking an organizational approach to training its believing members.

Let's look at the community oriented organizational approach to this follower training.

Follower Training

Jesus expertly and tenderly described the process for becoming his disciple to a village crowd outside Caesarea Philippi: "Whoever wants to be my disciple must deny themselves and take up their cross and follow me."[31] The early Church adhered to these straightforward but challenging steps to transform believers into mature followers. Transforming a new believer into a fit follower in the Church today should be no different. The Holy Spirit working among healthy, mature spiritual mentors guides this developmental process of maturing the believer. The key is to mature the believer in a generationally appropriate manner. Millennials are quick to spread the word on how your training center functions. They must be connected to, served by, and available to their community in real time, online, and through social media. Just ask them, "What would make your experience better?"

During the time that Christianity was at its peak, believer development was more serendipitous based upon a loose church structure. Traditionally, church members grew spiritually by attending Sunday School and a worship service, by attending a Sunday or Wednesday night program, and then by participating in a mission outreach. No formal construct existed, because it wasn't necessary. Church roles were burgeoning, and opportunities for service were available like selections on a cafeteria menu. Educational programs of Bible studies, marriage conferences, prayer seminars, and spiritual gifts inventories supplemented a believer's discipleship.

In addition, people who are fifty and older have lived a monastic Christology, one that is vertical, existing privately between the pilgrim and the Lord. These older Christians have taken ownership of their discipleship. For congregants of the Boomer generation, growing in faith has been a merger of the outer corporate Church experience and the inner monastic experience. Younger Christians have grown up in a society that encourages horizontal relationships. They require mentoring and coaching in community in order to grow in maturity. Attraction to a church body is based upon a dynamic community of believers who want to sit, study, train, and grow together.

The postmodern U.S. Church is in decline especially among mainline faith tribes. Being a Christian is no longer popular or prevalent in the U.S. The reputation of Christianity is diminishing. People are leaving "the faith that was once for all entrusted to God's holy people."[32] Is this falling away from the faith[33] a precursor to the end days described in the Bible?[34] Or have we grown idle and restless waiting on Christ's return?[35] In most churches, there are more Boomers than Millennials. Young people are spiritually curious, but their notion of faith doesn't align with that of traditionalists. Christians are receiving harsh media criticism because we are often perceived as acting in unChristian ways. Has our wickedness caused our love of the Lord to grow cold?[36]

Unchurched people are now rooted in a form of radical individualism. They are independent, self-absorbed, and skeptical of traditions. Most view church people as judgmental, hypercritical, and old-fashioned. Our troubles seem slight when compared to Christians in the time of Nero.[37] The apostle Paul tells us that the enemy has always been the devil.[38] "Everyone who wants to live a godly life in Christ Jesus will be persecuted."[39] This is a perfect time to come together in his churches, hold fast to his teachings, encourage our hearts, and strengthen in every good deed and word.[40] Like the early Christians, we have a real opportunity for service and evangelism.

Ordained and non-ordained leaders have an obligation to become spiritually fit so that they may lead their churches in building up the next generation of Christians. A more intentional, community-oriented approach that involves the holy characteristics of leadership, structure, and process is necessary to develop young believers into followers. Churches that become wellness-oriented and function like a spiritual fitness center have a chance to produce followers. When we look at our definition of fitness and the drivers for church wellness from the data presented, we see that Jesus wants not only followers, but also worthy or fit followers. These followers become enthusiasts in their churches, where they serve sacrificially.

The fitness lifestyle is augmented by creating an f✝s (follower training site), culture within your church. The atmosphere surrounding the church should be one that invites and welcomes the empowering presence of the Holy Spirit. The culture of the early church was one of excitement, togetherness, learning, and training about the Way. Creating a culture of growing faith and maturity for building up the Kingdom is the essential component of the follower training site. The f✝s is not a destination, but a charging station for even the fittest of saints to practice, to train, and to share their stories of running the race, climbing the mountain, and guiding others in the valley of life. More importantly, the f✝s is a gathering place where believers of all fitness levels can encourage, inspire, and motivate each other to build fitness in the Lord.

As a follower training site, the ekklesia fulfills its purpose by working in community to reproduce fit followers so the church can accomplish its vision. Its strength comes from a unanimous understanding between leaders, staff, and members about the church's purpose, focus, and mission. Organizationally, church leaders must provide the process for believers to reproduce into fit followers. Leadership can create the culture for members to grow with an open mind, obedient will, and united heart.

The pastor (or designee) should serve as the coach or head fitness trainer. The fitness instructors are selected, trained, and certified by the leadership team. Leaders must not capitulate and take shortcuts when building this spiritual fitness center.[41] Leaders should demonstrate the heart of Christ in all decisions. allowing members to have an inviting atmosphere in which to train. Changes will have to be made to the present construct and culture within most churches.

Proper nutrition is essential for the spiritual athlete in training. The role of the church is to provide the facility, fuel, worship setting, and Eucharist. The pastoral staff and church leaders should demonstrate servant leadership by setting the table, removing obstacles to worship, and maximizing the pathway toward a balanced spiritual diet.

The church provides the exercise equipment, and leadership provides the trainers so the Body's followers are built up and matured. Faith-building together in community is the common denominator in both work-in and workout sessions. By tithing time, labor, and money, trainees can reduce facility costs and add value to the center by contributing expertise (spiritual gifts), encouragement (faith), and inspiration (maturity) to everyone at the training center.

The underlying maintenance and management of the fitness facility depends upon the administration of the staff, pastor, and leadership. The leadership should demand a service-oriented staff that maintains an organized, clean, and up-to-date center. The church provides the exercise equipment, but the staff must keep it in working order. The exercise equipment is the organizational process of training its members.

Every church is imbued with assets, both material and organic. Leadership should make those assets accessible for member development and service. Churches with limited assets may have high member use (high asset turnover), but money and physical assets should not be a limiting factor for any ekklesia. Leadership should monitor turnover and make strategic changes to accommodate the needs of the center. Trainees should not compete for limited assets, nor delay training or service due to asset limitations.

The internal and external branding of this fitness center should be consistent. Leadership must develop the culture within the organization so that trainers, staff, and trainees reflect the essence and fragrance of Christ. Developing the Mind of Christ in your center (purpose, focus, passion, mission, and vision) makes decision-making, branding, and quality control easier.

With this fitness lifestyle, the organizational culture is already defined for your ekklesia. Your purpose is to love the Lord[42] and *win* the race.[43] Your focus is to bear fruit,[44] and your passion is to love others.[45] The ekklesia's vision is to reproduce and build up the next generation of fit followers by functioning as a desirable spiritual fitness center. How your church executes the fitness site and expresses the love of Christ is unique to each leadership and church. Altogether, the training site reproduces worthy followers to reach new converts, but understanding the next generation and how to reach them is of paramount importance to accomplishing the vision.

The chart on the next page summarizes the **Fitness Roles** within churches striving for a fitness lifestyle. The far-left column lists the different aspects of the fitness lifestyle. The corresponding roles for the church (f✝s), the leadership (coaches and trainers), and the members (trainees) are then compared on the right.

Fitness Lifestyle	Church's Role	Leader's Role	Member's Role
Culture	Holy Spirit	Mind of Christ	Train in community
Fuel: *PSF	Provide	Set the table	Balanced nutrition
Water	Worship	Excellence	Hydrate regularly
Vitamin	Communion	Pathway	Participate fully
Administration-Management	Staff/pastor/some leaders	Directs/monitors staff & pastor	Believer support
Exercise	Equipment/resources	Instructor(s)	Participants
Assets	Physical	Regulate turnover	Labor
	Intellectual	Vision directed	Time
	Spiritual	Fruit oriented	Train
	Financial	Manager	Giving and tithe
Purpose	WIN	Next generation	Run to get the prize
Focus	Bear fruit	Educate about spiritual gifts	Bear fruit using spiritual gifts
Passion	Touch hearts	Simulate Christ's love	Develop Christ's love
Vision	Build up fit followers	Equip trainers	Transform into fit followers
Mission	f✝s	Develop trainers	Do-BeDo

Fitness Roles

158

T⁵raining

Once the f✝s concept is created and adopted, church leaders can symbolically bring in the fitness equipment for each training station: the necessary people, study or training materials, and ministries used for teaching and training. The connectional and relational aspect of the f✝s is not to be underestimated. Process is very important. Mature believers, in some cases a remnant of enthusiasts, should be trained to serve as trainers. Their training is all about understanding the new construct of communal discipleship and communicating it to believers in training. These trainers serve as facilitators and guides for the trainees exercising their new faith. Trainers remain in the background while young believers train in community. Training is understanding the Way. Training is growing in Christ intimacy. Training is sharing in faith victories and in life's failures together. Training is learning to be dependent upon our only source of real strength: Jesus Christ. Training is understanding the significance of the cross and the personal substitutionary sacrifice of the Savior.

The letter "T" stands for training, but it is also symbolic of the cross on which Jesus shed his blood and died. Each training station strengthens different muscles exposed to the love, grace, and mercy of our Lord. True, there are five training stations. But T⁵ also expresses the exponential power of each station upon the follower in training; therefore, it is transformational.

The **T⁵** concept involves five fitness-training stations where believers exercise their salvation, become apprentices in discipleship, learn obedience, and mature in their faith. The five T's are Together, Table, Teach, Train, and Touch. Believers at the various **T⁵** stations, Sit, Study, Serve, and Share, are within a like-minded community of participants who want to transform into mature, fit followers. The fitness stations develop the two basic postures of follower fitness: *Being* in Christ and *Doing* (serving) with Christ. **T⁵** training unleashes a spiritual chain reaction to accomplish the will of God within his churches.

To demonstrate the complex organizational dynamics within a fitness Body acting like a spiritual fitness center, let's study how a fit church uses **T⁵** to accomplish its vision of building up fit followers (or "BUFF"). The following diagram may help to visualize the concept.

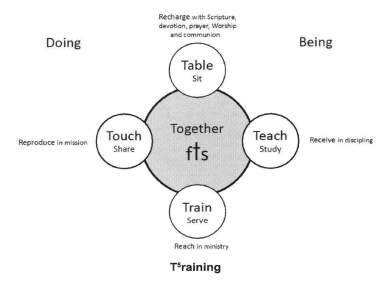

For a believer in training, the diagram can be divided into two sides of spiritual training: *Being* in Christ (on the right side) and *Doing* with Christ (on the left side). Deep personal relationships among believers working in community (or "WIC") augment the Holy Spirit to build up other followers in training. When a community of followers leaves their church to share the gospel with their neighbors in the world (working out of community, or "WOC"), the next generation of people comes to know the one true Lord. These "work-ins" and "workouts" take place in the present tense where hearts are shared and shaped in Christ's image. During T^5, the passing of time in community is importantly structured in terms of WIC WOC, WIC WOC.

Paul constantly preached a mutuality or common unity among believers. He said that in the Church, Christians should have a unified purpose.[46] The members of the Body should be mutually dependent as they exercise distinctive functions.[47] Unity is not created, but is the holy by-product of believers growing and maturing in community.[48] Manifestation of the Spirit is given to them for a common goal.[49] Unity is organic, whereby all believers are one in heart and mind.[50] It is recreative of relationships through warm acceptance and understanding in a mutually supportive environment.

Paul says to respect those who are over you in the Lord and to encourage one another and build each other up.[51] "Being one in Spirit and of one mind."[52] Togetherness is in the center of the diagram and at the center of ecclesia transformation. Like the CrossFit experience discussed earlier, believer development is done together in community. The Body improves its faith fitness through *being* and *doing*; therefore, the fit heartbeat of the f✝s is do-bedo, do-bedo, do-bedo.[53]

The ekklesia's heartbeat gets stronger as followers train and become more fit in community.[54] This paradigm speaks to both unchurched and to believing Millennials! The apostle Paul says, "This mystery is that through the gospel the Gentiles are heirs together with Israel, members together of one body, and sharers together in the promise in Christ Jesus."[55] The mystery of discipleship takes place under the conditions of God's children growing and maturing in the gospel together. The paradox of spiritual maturity is that believers are the freest when they are bound in the discipline of the gospel.[56]

To work in community means trainees sit, study, and serve together. The Body's trainers provide the table, teaching, and training so that trainees develop into followers. Trainees sit together at the symbolic table that only a renewed church can provide to its committed and uncommitted believers so that they may be recharged through corporate worship, communion, Scripture, prayer, and fellowship, the important fuels of development.[57]

Trainees experience spiritual maturity by participating in discipling and shepherding programs where mature followers teach the Christian virtues spoken of by the apostle Peter.[58] *Being* in community and working in ministry trains members to understand the supernatural power of God's love acted out in the life of fellow believers. *Being* in community helps followers observe the ways of God, understand the nature of God, and observe God's work in the lives of others.[59]

Working and training in community together grows faith, maturity, obedience, and followership. Younger generations like Mosaics or Millennials (born between 1981 and 1996) have a keen interest in learning more about the Bible and training; therefore, *Being* in community may be a good church entry point for younger generations.

Being and *doing* are uniquely integrated in the fts when believers learn to serve in ministry within the Church. Being a disciple means being an apprentice, for an apprentice must practice what he or she has been taught. The apostle James says, "Do not merely listen to the word, and so deceive yourselves. Do what it says."[60] Followers require the proper tools and training in order to *do* the ministries of the Church well. Performing ministry among fellow followers-in-training prepares and sharpens believers' skills for the rigors of sharing the heart of Christ to unbelievers in the world. Too often, a church sends out its people to represent the heart of Christ, only to discover they are not ready for such a task. Proper follower development is necessary to share the fragrance of our Lord. Our witness must be representative of the heart of Christ, not an afflicted version of oneself.

Faith Fitness uses the human body as a template for a church's body of believers. The church body is made fit with leaders who provide the resources to train believers in an intentional, community-oriented culture to become enthusiastic followers. A fit Body practices lifestyle habits that limit afflictions and encourage service.

> This is to my Father's glory,
> that you bear much fruit,
> showing yourselves to be my disciples.
> John[61]

Fitness Moment

- The functioning of the church organization has many parallels to the human body.
- The muscles of a church are its fit followers. By building up the muscles, the deeds and work of the church can be accomplished.
- A fit Body uses fitness habits within the Church to reproduce fit followers.
- The fit followers share the love of Christ both inside and outside the church. They accomplish the vision, mission, and purpose of their church.
- Leadership is essential in creating the processes, equipment, training stations, and community-oriented culture of the spiritual fitness center.
- The essential desire of a fit Body is sharing the gospel of Jesus Christ, evangelism, and Kingdom building. Remember, fitness means passing the ecclesial DNA of Christ to the next generation.
- The last prescription is to run the race!

Run the Race

Sig: *follow the instructions*
Refill(s): *prn – as needed*
Comments: *No substitutions permitted*

Do you not know that in a race all the runners run,
but only one gets the prize?
Run in such a way as to get the prize.
Apostle Paul[62]

My favorite Scripture that applies to the believer living in community and in the world as a fit follower is in the book of Hebrews. "Therefore, since we are surrounded by such a great cloud of witnesses, let us throw off everything that hinders and the sin that so easily entangles. And let us run with perseverance the race marked out for us."[63] Every generation has Christians who have trained to become mature disciples and who have become heroes of the faith.

I enjoyed playing sports as a child. I remember being awed by the Olympics. We all remember the greatest and most memorable winning moments in Olympic history, like Kerri Strug's gold medal gymnastic vault in the 1996 Atlanta games. The vignette of the athlete who "came up short" but demonstrated incredible character in their attempt has always been my favorite Olympic moment.

Somehow these tragic moments are bizarrely uplifting. Many such stunning Olympic moments exist, but the most powerful to me was Derek Redmond in the 1992 Barcelona games. You can watch the "You Raise Me Up" version of this incredible moment on YouTube.[64]

Derek was the poster child of fitness, and he was favored to win the 400-meter race that year. Everything he had done in his life pointed like a laser to that one moment. The race began uneventfully. Derek was running the race of his lifetime until 250 meters from the finish, when his hamstring muscle suddenly tore from its insertion site, leaving Derek grasping the back of his leg. In crisis mode, bewildered and not understanding what had happened, Derek hobbled to a stop and collapsed to the track surface. Competitors flew by him. His mind slowly caught up to the devastating implication that, for all practical purposes, his race was over.

Derek Redmond's heart then processed what his body already knew. Time stood still while, grimacing and crying, Derek rose and turned toward the finish line. As the last competitor finished the race, Derek waved off help from officials. He wanted to finish alone. The anguish on his face as he determinedly began hopping drew the cameras closer to this public tragedy. Now 68,000 stadium spectators and a world of viewers focused their attention on a real-life drama unfolding before their eyes.

After an excruciating 50 meters, Derek was slowed again on the track, only this time it was the crucible of pain, disappointment, and raw emotion that overwhelmed his body. Just as this human wreck was losing all hope, a lone man fought through race security to help. The rescuer received more than Derek's bodily weight when Derek collapsed in his grasp. The supporter who offered himself for succor and strength was Derek's father. The father lifted up his son, encouraging him, "Finish your race, son."

Recognizing the turn of events, the crowd began cheering encouragement. Buoyed by the support, Derek's father released him 50 meters from the finish.

Derek crossed the finish line to a standing ovation. Despite his condition, Derek finished the race.

Derek's race is a portrait of *optimal* fitness and of the faith fitness movement. We can't do it alone either. We need our Father to support, guide, and encourage us. Despite any adversity or affliction, your ekklesia can train for the race, run the race, and contribute to the Kingdom. God can use us despite our human limitations or lack of understanding, because he has supernatural plans. Derek won his race, and our ekklesias can win, too.

The usual reward for being a top finisher in any type of game is a prize. God has prepared a similar reward system for believers. Paul described his prize to the Philippians when he said, "I press on toward the goal to win the prize for which God has called me heavenward in Christ Jesus."[65] Then he motivated the Corinthians to run with purpose: "Do you not know that in a race all the runners run, but only one gets the prize? Run in such a way as to get the prize."[66] Beyond the ultimate prize awarded in heaven, the rewards of ministry are many. Fellowship, team unity, personal growth, intimacy with Jesus Christ, and that fit feeling of well-being are just a few.

Many Christians sit in the stands or on sidelines and watch the game of life pass them by. God wants you on the field of life participating, growing, giving, and enjoying. Notice that the author of Hebrews says, "let us throw off everything that hinders and the sin that so easily entangles." We must stay focused, remain healthy, and realize our state of optimal fitness in order to run the race. Paul appealed to the Galatians to stay single-minded during their work when he said, "You were running a good race. Who cut in on you to keep you from obeying the truth?"[67]

For church leadership, the fitness lifestyle resembles the regimen of followers "in-training" within the spiritual fitness center. Believers train among like-minded trainees who have adopted the same discipline, vision, and goals. They learn how to overcome obstacles, trials, hardship, and temptation. Social media, virtual church, streaming services, and church apps are no longer intimidating. Reaching younger generations and making relevant connections with community is again exciting, joyful, and rewarding. The ekklesia is systematically reproducing worthy fit followers, while believers are training enthusiastically. The trainers at the fitness center provide direction, mentoring, and maturing. The head coach (the ordained leader) communicates the Mind of Christ while the trainers (lay leadership) communicate the heart of Christ to the community.

Faith Fitness is all about creating a culture of spiritual health and growing in faith as a community of believers who fulfill the purpose of their church. Follower development becomes the by-product of this follower fitness culture. Like the elite Olympic athlete, training prepares followers to enter the new moraine of a harsh world with the confidence of Christ, the playing field of life, to run the race marked out before us. A trained follower becomes attuned to the whisper of the Lord. He or she can hear him say, "Whom shall I send? And who will go for us?" The fit follower says, "I am ready. Here am I. Send me!"[68]

Glossary

Body – The membership of God's holy churches.

BUFF – Acronym for Building Up Fit Followers, the vision for churches using the Fitness Model.

Church Rx – The prescription for churches.

Community – The membership of a church *being* and *doing* together.

Ekklesia – The New Testament name for an assembly of believers forming a church. "Eecclesia" may also be used interchangeably and is usually used as an adjective.

Enthusiast – A church member who contains the zeal of the Holy Spirit, understands the importance of reaching the next generation and participates fully in the purpose and mission of their church.

Fitness – A believer or church leader who takes ownership of their spiritual development and who adapts to the environment to build up and to plant the gospel in the next generation of believers.

Fitness Body – Demonstrates the most important parts of the church—Christ, the head; Mind of Christ, the heart; clergy/staff, the central nervous system; lay leadership, the cardiovascular system; members, the muscles; hands and feet—with their interrelated functions.

Fitness Driver – An essential function without which a church cannot achieve a state of Christ-like fitness.

Fitness Lifestyle – A church that creates a culture of ongoing training to accomplish the vision, mission, and purpose of that church.

Fit Follower – A follower who trains in community for the purpose of running the race to build up the next generation of followers.

Follower – A believer who strives for intimacy with Christ and works to grow in maturity.

Follower Training Site or f✝s – A church that wants to internally brand its vision and mission by becoming a spiritual fitness center for the purpose of bringing worthy spiritual fitness, unity, maturity, and service to its membership.

Free-rider – A member who attends for personal gain but does not give of their time, labor, money, or evangelism.

Health – The way a church perceives its functionality based upon limitations caused by disease(s) from sin, self, and Satan.

Marginal Cost – The cost to the church (in administrative time, labor, and money) of having one more person or family join the church as a full member.

Mind of Christ – The most important driver of church fitness, representing the heart and soul of the church established by the biblical metaphors of the Bride, the Branch, and the Body, whereby a relevant vision, mission, and purpose become the core of all decision-making.

Optimal Fitness – A fit believer or ekklesia who gives all to Christ despite any limitations.

Patient – A sample church representing any mainline or declining faith tribe.

Ruach – A Hebrew word meaning "Spirit." The Aramaic also suggests "breath" or "spirit." A Ruach is a spiritual exercise or workout performed in community to breath in the Holy Spirit so that Christ reigns over the heart of the believer to perfect the love of Christ in his or her life.

Strictness – A term that an academic researcher, Iannaconne, uses to describe a church who demands complete loyalty, unwavering belief, and adherence to a distinctive lifestyle.

T⁵ransformation – The church functioning as a spiritual fitness center uses the combination of togetherness, table, teaching, training, and touching to mysteriously mature and transform believers into fit followers. In community, trainees sit at Christ's table for communion, prayer, and worship, study the

Word of God, train to serve as shepherds and ministers, and share the love of Christ by touching others in the world. As believers participate by being in community and by doing with community, they transform into people who understand the mission of their church.

Wellness – The condition of good spiritual health as a result of the ekklesia taking ownership of their condition with leadership that provides the proper nutrition, exercise, and training habits.

WIN – An acronym describing the purpose of followers: Work our lives Into the lives of our Neighbors.

Workout – The description of believers exercising and training in community. Also referred to as "work-ins," because the exercises occur within community.

Appendix 1:

Modern-Day Theologian Book References

Callahan, Kennon L., 1987. *Twelve Keys to an Effective Church*, San Francisco, Harper & Row, p. 14: Twelve Central Characteristics of an Effective Church.

Barna, George, 1990. *The Frog in the Kettle*, Ventura, California, Regal, p. 226: Ten Critical, Achievable Goals. . . for the 90s.

MacArthur, John, 1990. *Marks of a Healthy Church*, Chicago, Moody Press, p. 23: Marks of an Effective Church.

Barna, George, 1991. *User Friendly Churches*, Ventura, California, Regal: Ten Things Successful User-friendly Churches Don't Do.

Shelley, Bruce and Shelley, Marshall, 1992. *The Consumer Church*, Downers Grove, Ill, Intervarsity, p. 226: Seven Vital Steps to Create a Healthy Blend of Effectiveness and Faithfulness.

Barna, George, 1993. *Turn-Around Churches*, Ventura, California, Regal, p. 42: Eleven Factors of Dying Churches Revived, or Restored to Wholeness.

Rainer, Thom, 1993. *The Book of Church Growth*, Nashville, Broadman & Holman, pp. 171-316: Thirteen Principles of Church Growth.

Grudem, Wayne, 1994. *Systematic Theology*, Grand Rapids, Michigan, Zondervan: Twelve Signs of a More Pure Church.

Hemphill, Ken, 1994. *The Antioch Effect: Eight Characteristics of Highly Effective Churches*, Nashville, Broadman & Holman.

Stewart, Carlyle Fielding, 1994. *African American Church Growth*, Nashville, Abingdon: Twelve Principles for Prophetic Ministry.

Rainer, Thom, 1995. *Giant Awakenings*, Nashville, Broadman & Holman: Nine Surprising Trends that Can benefit Your Church.

Warren, Rick, 1995. *The Purpose Driven Church*, Grand Rapids, Michigan, Zondervan, pp. 49, 103-107: Five Purposes Statement and Program for Church Growth.

Wagner, Peter C., 1996. *The Healthy Church: Avoiding and Curing the Nine Diseases that Can Afflict Any Church*, Ventura, California, Regal.

Woods, Jeff C., 1996. *Congregational Megatrends*, Washington, D.C., Albans Institute: Seven Megatrends Happening in Congregations.

Hull, Bill, 1997. *Seven Steps to Transform Your Church*, Grand Rapids, Michigan, Revell.

Robinson, Darrell W., 1997. *Total Church Life*, Nashville, Broadman & Holman, p. 4: Twelve Components of Total Church Life Strategy.

Shaw, Mark, 1997. *Ten Great Ideas from Church History*, Downers Grove, Ill, Intervarsity.

White, James Emery, 1997; 2nd ed., 2003. *Rethinking the Church*, Grand Rapids, Michigan, Baker.

Barna, George, 1998. *The Habits of Highly Effective Churches*, Ventura, California, Regal.

McLaren, Brian D., 1998. *Reinventing Your Church*, Grand Rapids, Michigan, Zondervan: Thirteen Strategies.

Schwarz, Christian A., 1998. *The ABC's of Natural Church Development*, Carol Stream, Illinois, ChurchSmart: Eight Quality Characteristics of Growing Churches.

Anderson, Leith, Winter 1999. "Seven Ways to Rate Your Church," *Leadership*: What People are Looking For.

Bisagno, John, 1999. "Five Characteristics of Successful Churches" (unpublished sermon).

Galloway, Dale E., 1999. *Making Church Relevant*, Kansas City, Missouri, Beacon Hill: Ten Characteristics of a Healthy Church, Plus One.

Macchia, Stephen, 1999. *Becoming a Healthy Church*, Grand Rapids, Michigan, Baker: Ten Characteristics.

MacNair, Donald, J., 1999. *The Practices of a Healthy Church*, Phillipsburg, New Jersey, Presbyterian & Reformed: Three Vital Signs, Six Healthy Practices.

Dever, Mark, 2000. *Nine Marks of a Healthy Church*, Wheaton, Illinois, Crossway.

Gibbs, Eddie, 2000. *Church Next*, Downers Grove, Illinois, Intervarsity Press, p. 52 citing *The Gospel and Our Culture* 10, no. 3 [1998]: Twelve Empirical Indicators of a Missional Church.

Miller, Herb, 2000. "What Priorities Build a Healthy Church?", The MBA Connection, Parish Paper: Four Main Priorities, What Else Counts—Eight More Priorities.

Russell, Bob, 2000. *When God Builds a Church: Ten Principles for Growing A Dynamic Church*, West Monroe, Louisiana, Howard.

2000. Report of the Plenary of the Consultation of Church Union: Nine Visible Marks of Churches Uniting in Christ.

Baake, Robert, 2001. "Ten Leading Indicators of a Healthy Church," EFCA *Beacon*, p. 13.

Rainer, Thom, April 17, 2001. "Nine Habits to Attract, Keep Unchurched," *Western Recorder*, p. 10.

Stetzer, Ed, February 27, 2001. "Prof Lists Ten Commandments for Post Modern U.S. Churches," *Western Recorder*, p. 7.

Werning, Waldo, 2001. *Twelve Pillars of a Healthy Church*, St. Charles, Illinois, ChurchSmart.

Stanley, Andy and Young, Ed, 2002. *Can We Do That? Twenty-Four Innovative Practices that will Change the Way You Do Church*, West Monroe, Louisiana, Howard.

McIntosh, Gary L., 2003. *Biblical Church Growth*, Grand Rapids, Michigan, Baker.

Ryken, Philip Graham, 2003. *City on a Hill*, Chicago, Moody Press.

Scazzero, Peter, 2003. *The Emotionally Healthy Church*, Grand Rapids, Michigan, Zondervan.

Garrison, David, 2003. *Church Planting Movements*, Midlothian, Virginia, WIGTake Resources.

Appendix 2:

Church Factors from Academic Studies

Category	Church Factors	Publication
Context: National, institutional	Conservative sects	Kelley '72; Roof et al '79;
	societal, and external contributors	McKinney '79; Fink & Stark '92; Iannaccone '92; Marcum '10
	Denominational affiliation	Roozen & Hadaway '93
	Independent churches	Bradley et al '92
	Religious resources	Olson '89; Iannaccone '95
	New Evangelical Movement	Perrin et al '97
	Population growth/new housing	Roozen & Hadaway '93
	Rural/Southern location	Roozen & Hadaway '93
	Small churches	Roozen & Hadaway '93
	Member resources	Zaleski & Zech '95; Iannaccone '95
	Low birth rate—female members	Hout et al '01
	Optimal size/older clergy/ costs	Zaleski & Zech '95; Barna '09
Program: Organization structure, plans and activities	Small groups	Dudley & Cummings '83
	Church school size	Thompson et al '93
	Education emphasis	Thompson et al '93
	Extensiveness of programs	Roozen '04
	Contemporary worship	Roozen '04
	Children/youth focus/ programs	Roozen '08
	Specialty programs	Roozen '08

Identity: Beliefs, values, style, and stories	Conservative beliefs	Hayward '05
	Traditional beliefs	Hoge et al '93
	Strict beliefs	Kelley '72; Tamney et al '03
	Strict beliefs eliminate "free riders"	Iannaccone '92, '94
	Presence of Holy Spirit in worship	Roozen '08
	Spiritual practices	Roozen '04
	Church participation	Dougherty '04; Woolever & Bruce '04
	Newer worshipers/percent new	Bruce et al '06; Woolever & Bruce '04
	Worship attendance and contributions	Iannaccone '95
	Incr. ratio of attendance at worship/member	Medcalfe & Sharp '12
	Female members	Hadaway '06
	Absence of predominantly white members	Hadaway '06
	Friendships	Olson '89
	Caring for children/youth	Woolever & Bruce '04
Process: Leadership, decision making, problem solving, and conflict management	Positive outlook for future	Thompson et al '93
	Leadership/vision/mission/ purpose/training	Bruce et al '06; Roozen '08; De Weter et al '10
	Losing members	Medcalfe & Sharp '12
	Use of spiritual gifts to build commitment	Roozen & Hadaway '93
	Increasing spiritual vitality	Bruce et al '06; Roozen '08; De Weter '10
	Beliefs lead to commitment	Roozen & Hadaway '93
	Small groups build commitment	Roozen & Hadaway '93
	Organizational commitment/ identification	Wilson et al '93
	Making converts into Enthusiasts/stem losses	Hayward '05; Hadaway '06; Roozen '08

176

Identified givers in contributions	Medcalfe & Sharp '12
Pastor compensation per member	Medcalfe & Sharp '12
Self-focus on faith, growth, service = negative	Woolever & Bruce '04
Absence of conflict in worship, leadership, and finances	Roozen '04

Appendix 3

Academic Research References

Barna, G., "How faith varies by church size," The Barna Group, 2009.

Bradley, Martin B., Green, Norman M. Jr., Jones, Dale, Lynn, Mac, and McNeil, Lou, *Churches and Church Membership in the United States 1990*, (Atlanta: Glenmary Research Center, 1992).

Bruce, D., Woolever, C., Wulff, K., & Smith-Williams, I., "Fast-growing churches: What distinguishes them from others?" *Journal of Beliefs and Values*, 2006, 27(1), 111-126.

De Wetter, C., Gochman, I., Luss, R. and Sherwood, R. "UMC call to action: Vital congregations research project," 2010, Towers Watson.

Doughtery, K.D.,"Institutional Influences on Growth in Southern Baptist congregations," *Review of Religious Research*, 2004, 46:117-131.

Dudley, R.L. and Cummings, D., "Study of factors relating to church growth in the North American Division of the Seventh-Day Adventists," *Review of Religious Research*, 1983, 24(4), 322-333.

Finck, R. and Stark, R., *The Churching of America, 1776-1990: Winners and Losers in America's Religious Economy*, (Rutgers University Press, 1992).

Finke, Roger, and Stark, Rodney, *The Churching of America, 1776-1990: Winners and Losers in America's Religious Economy*, (Rutgers University Press, 1992).

Hadaway, C. Kirk, "Is Evangelistic Activity Related to Church Growth?", pp. 169-87 in *Church and Denominational Growth: What does (and Does Not) Cause Growth and Decline,* edited by David A. Roozen and C. Kirk Hadaway (Abingdon Press, 1993).

Hadaway, C.K. and Roozen, D. A., "The Growth and Decline of Congregations," in D.A. Roozen and C.K. Hadaway (Eds) *Church and Denominational Growth* (Nashville, Tennessee: Abingdon Press, 1993), 127-134.

Hayward, J., "A General Model of Church Growth and Decline," *Journal of Mathematical Sociology*, 2005, 29, 177-207.

Hoge, D.R. and Roozen, D.A. (eds), *Understanding Church Growth and Decline: 1950-1978*, (New York: Pilgrims Press, 1979).

Hoge, D.R., Benton, J. and Luidens, D., *Vanishing Boundaries*, (Louisville, Kentucky: Westminster John Knox Press, 1993).

Hout, M., Greely, A. and Wilde, M., "The Decline of the Mainline: the demographic imperative," *American Journal of Sociology*, 2001, 107, 468-500.

Iannaccone, Laurence R., "Sacrifice and Stigma: Reducing Free-Riding in Cults, Communes, and other Collectives," *Journal of Political Economy*, 1992, 100:271-92.

Iannaccone, L.R., Olson, D.V.A., & Stark, R., "Religious resources and church growth," *Social Forces*, 1995, 74(2), 705-731.

Iannaccone, Laurence R., "Why Strict Churches Are Strong," *American Journal of Sociology*, 1994, 99:1180-1211.

Iannaccone, Laurence R., "Religious Resources and Church Growth," *Social Forces*, 1995, 74, 2: 704-725.

Kelly, Dean, *Why Conservative Churches Are Growing: A Study in the Sociology of Religion with a New Preface for the ROSE Edition*, (Mercer University Press, 1896 [1972]).

Marcum, Jack, "Membership Change in the Presbyterian Church (USA): Trends in Gains and Losses," *Comparative Statistics*, 2009, 1-4.

McKinney, W. J., "Performance of United Church of Christ congregations in Massachusetts and Pennsylvania," 224-247 in D. Hoge and D. Roozen (eds.), *Understanding Church Growth and Decline: 1950-1978*, (New York: Pilgrim Press, 1979).

Medcalfe and Sharp, "Enthusiasm and Congregational Growth: Evidence from the United Methodist Church," *International Journal of Business and Social Science*, Vol. 3 No.9, May 2012.

Olson, D.V.A., "Church friendships: Boon or barrier to church growth?" *Journal for the Scientific Study of Religion*, 1989, 28(4), 432-447.

Perrin, R. D., Kennedy, P. and Miller, D. E., "Examining sources of conservative church growth: Where are the new evangelical movements getting their numbers?" *Journal for the Scientific Study of Religion*, 1997, 36(1), 71-80.

Roof, W. C., Hoge, D., Dyble, J., and Hadaway, C.K., "Factors producing growth or decline in United Presbyterian congregations," 198-223 in D. Hoge and D. Roozen (eds.), *Understanding Church Growth and Decline: 1950-1978*, (New York: Pilgrim Press, 1979).

Roozen, D.A., *Oldline Protestantism: pockets of vitality within a continuing stream of decline* (Hartford, Connecticut: Hartford Institute for Religion research, 2004), available online at: http://hirr.hartsem.edu/bookshelf/oozen_article5.html (accessed November 2010).

Roozen, David A., *American Congregations 2008: FACT- Faith Communities Today*, (Hartford, Connecticut: Hartford Institute for Religion Research, 2009), 1-37.

Roozen, David A., and Hadaway, C. Kirk (eds.), *Church and Denominational Growth: What does (and Does Not) Cause Growth or Decline*, (Nashville, Tennessee: Abingdon Press, 1993).

Tamney, J. B., Johnson, S. D., McElmurry, K., and Saunders, G., "Strictness and Congregational Growth In Middletown," *Journal for the Scientific Study of Religion*, 2003, 42, 363-375.

Thompson, W. L., Carroll, J. W., and Hoge, D. R., "Growth or Decline in Presbyterian Congregations," in D. A. Roozen & C. K. Hadaway (eds.), *Church and Denominational Growth*, (Nashville, Tennessee: Abingdon Press, 1993), 188-207.

Weems, Lovett H., Jr., Arnold, Joseph E., and Michel, Ann A., "A Lewis Center Report: Clergy Age Trends in the United Methodist Church 1985-2009," Wesley Theological Seminary, Lewis Center for Church Leadership, p. 1-6, accessed March 20, 2010: http://www.churchleadership.com/research/um_clergy_age_trends09.htm.

Wilson, Gerald L., Keyton, Joann, Johnson, G. David, Geiger, Cheryl, and Clark, Johanna C., "Church Growth Through Member Identification and Commitment: a Congregational Case Study," *Review of Religious Research*, 1993, Volume: 34, Issue: 3, 259., obtained via Questia online library, November 3, 2010: http://www.questia.com/reader/printPaginator/1203.

Woolever, C. and Bruce, D., *Beyond the Ordinary: Ten Strengths of US Congregations*, (Louisville, Kentucky: Westminster John Knox Press, 2004).

Zaleski, Peter, Zech, Charles, "The Optimal Size of a Religious Congregation: An Economic Theory of Clubs Analysis," *The American Journal of Economics and Sociology*, 1995, 54:439-453.

Appendix 4

Fitness Exercises

The Journey Ruach

These prescriptive exercises specifically address the spiritual heart of church leaders and their ekklesia. After leadership fully participates in the prescriptive process, they will be ready to complete a strategy for ascending the fitness spectrum.

Proverbs 4:20-22 says, "My son, pay attention to what I say; turn your ear to my words. Do not let them out of your sight, keep them within your heart; for they are life to those who find them and health to one's whole body." The principles within the Scripture capture the ingredients of following directions: paying attention, listening carefully, and having a teachable attitude. There are no shortcuts for restoring the fortunes of your church or for transforming the heart of your assembly. Seasoned leaders, who have lived in the crucible of church life, have little time to read *Faith Fitness*. Most leaders say, "Just give me the ingredients of the secret sauce."

Your church can't elevate its level of fitness overnight. Attaining a fit church culture is a process that requires prayer, God's intervention, and fit leadership. The prescriptions rest, reflection, repentance, renewal and recommitment, respond, and run the race followed in succession will help transform your Body into enthusiasts for Christ. Under God's authority with mortar and pestle of the Word, the prescriptions have been carefully compounded to bring healing, renewal, and a fitness lifestyle to your assembly.

1. What is teachability? Describe each of the components of being teachable. How can church leaders model this important trait?

   Change culture in book

2. Do you believe that the Lord Jesus Christ, the Great Physician, can heal your spiritual afflictions? Do you want to be healed? Explain.

3. Do you want to become a worthy follower of Jesus? Does anything scare you about a renewed heart? Why should we not be afraid?

4. Meet with your clergy person, and invite him/her to participate in this journey with you. Detail the benefits.

5. Invite other church leaders to participate in this journey. Attempt to have your entire leadership participate.

Rx: Rest Ruach

The journey in *Faith Fitness* is special because we're taking it with those we love, Jesus Christ and other church leaders, and we're learning about the purpose and function of your church in the Kingdom. Packing is simple. We're only taking the book *Faith Fitness* and our Bible. Go at your own pace. Soak in the vista. Enjoy the journey. But like many adventures, don't underestimate the difficulty!

The mountain Annapurna in the Himalayas means "provider." Climber Ed Viesturs interpreted the meaning to understand that the mountain could provide for the mountaineer, if he would listen. Mountains have significance in the Bible. Saul and his three sons died on Mt. Gilboa.[1] Elijah defeated Baal's prophets on Mt. Carmel.[2] Moses was presented with the Ten Commandments on Mt. Sinai.[3] Joshua built an altar to God on Mt. Ebal.[4] Moses climbed Mt. Nebo so the Lord could show him the land God promised to Abraham, Isaac, and Jacob.[5] Christ was crucified on Golgotha.[6]

In Mark 6:31-32, Jesus said to his apostles, "'Come with me by yourselves to a quiet place and get some rest.' So they went away by themselves in a boat to a solitary place." In Matthew 11:28, Jesus told the people, "Come to me, all you who are weary and burdened, and I will give you rest." During our journey, the prescription to rest gives us permission to pause and go to the Lord in prayer and contemplation. In fact, the concept of "resting in the Lord" is a continuous act that gives the journey its spiritual focus. During our climb of understanding, we must never lose sight of the purpose of our study: to become fit leaders for the Lord.

1. What are the leadership challenges within the church today? What is your goal for taking this journey?

2. Describe conditions that would interfere with your ability to take this journey. Can you leave your baggage, especially church baggage, at home while on this fitness journey? Why or why not? Discuss as a group.

3. Historically, what is the greatest challenge that your church has faced? Is your church facing an Annapurna now?

4. Meet with leadership in your church and discuss the importance process of resting in the Lord while doing this study.

5. Keep a journal. Record your thoughts while you rest in the Lord.

Church Culture: Archetype Ruach

Church leaders tend to point to their local churches with the largest congregations as examples of the "ideal" church. These churches have certain advantages over smaller churches because of their size: higher revenues, more assets, higher leverage (borrowing), select ordained leaders, etc. Leaders often confuse size with health, wellness, or fitness among churches. As an ekklesia, we may not be called to be large. But we should be healthy, practice wellness principles, and strive for fitness.

The best place to look for examples of a healthy ekklesia is in the New Testament. In *Faith Fitness*, the churches of Smyrna, Philadelphia, and Thessalonica were discussed. Every church has obstacles, external and or internal, to overcome or control. These churches were no exception. Some church historians may say that the early church had many more obstacles as compared to modern-day churches. Some of these obstacles are mirrored on the mission field today.

To be a fit body of Christ, we must be functional and present with him. Leadership must control internal and external forces with the direction and help of the Lord. By being true to the Word of God and surrendering to Christ wholly, the church Body might come to know the will of God for their ekklesia. Only then can ordained and non-ordained leadership direct the Body to do his work in the Kingdom.

The fruit of works defines the future of the Church and every church. Despite limitations that each church may face, optimal fitness is possible. The assignment for church leadership is to build an organization that can accomplish the ingredients of a healthy ekklesia and fit church archetype. Every church should strive for this condition. Membership, church location, or depth of assets cannot limit the Almighty.

1. What are the characteristics that distinguish the five Revelation churches from the three healthy New Testament churches?

2. List the healthy ingredients that are present in your church. Rank them from most to least.

3. Which obstacle(s) may be limiting your church from having all the ingredients it needs?

4. Discuss how your leadership can incorporate the ingredients that are not as strong in your church.

5. Compare the healthy church archetype to the unhealthy archetypes. Describe the differences.

Church Culture: Fitness Spectrum Ruach

Ownership of a church's fitness condition belongs to its leadership. For most Christians, leadership is on-the-job training. In some churches, just being "active" qualifies members for a leadership position. The apostle Paul wrote letters of instruction to young church leaders to help them deal with problems in the early Church. In addition, various leaders like Timothy were sent to help guide growing ekklesias.

Many ordained clergy continue to proclaim that great preaching increases our church rolls. Others say that a robust music or youth program is the key. Those arguments are no longer valid. Now church leaders must build a culture that warms the Holy Spirit, gives purpose to the membership, and creates an inviting place for all generations.

The fact is that our churches move along a spectrum of organizational fitness that includes nominal, languid, well, or fit. Labelling churches can be harmful if not used for correction. Why seek to understand the level of fitness among church organizations except to improve their function? In evaluating a church organization, concepts like member enthusiasm, fit followers, faith, works, evangelism, and the presence of the Holy Spirit are all important.

Improving their level of fitness is a worthy goal for any church. Changing church culture is also essential, however. Nominal churches need leaders with hearts for Christ. Languid churches must educate leaders on how to develop processes to draw and grow new members into fit followers. Well churches should study and discern the proper strategy to birth, plant, or build new churches. If systems are in place to disciple members, to control conflict, and to grow outward or upward, then leadership will enjoy faith fitness.

1.   What are the four categories of church health that the author describes? Break into groups and discuss the nomenclature and the categories. Can you offer any substitutes?

2.   Jesus used the term "dead" to describe one of the Revelation churches. Which one? Why? Discuss the nominal church. Is it fair to categorize a church as nominal?

3.   Jesus also criticized four other Revelation churches. In each, faith or works or both were compromised. Describe the languid church. What are the similarities between a languid church today and these four Revelation churches?

4.   Describe the characteristics of a well church and a fit church. Distinguish between a well church and a languid or a nominal church.

5.   Review the Church Fitness Spectrum Chart. Where does your church fall on the spectrum? Discuss.

Rx: Reflection Ruach

According to Merriam-Webster.com, one definition of the word "reflection" is "a thought, idea, or opinion formed or a remark made as a result of meditation." Another is "an effect produced by an influence." The purpose of this prescription is to deal with your church's past and to look to the future while living in the present. Write down your thoughts, and list them in specific categories like the following: strengths, weaknesses, good memories, bad or traumatic memories, your role, if any, in those memories, any church behavior that may have been displeasing to God, and the vision and purpose of the church's future.

Time in reflection is intimate time with the Lord, who gives us permission to remember.[7] Reflection is not for fixing the past, building a strategy for the future, or solving problems. It is a time of honest deliberation and transparency that documents church life.

The next prescription allows ample opportunity to address past memories and sins. For now, count the blessings of good memories and face the bad memories and behaviors. The Great Physician will help you put them into perspective, release them unto him, and free you and your church from their bondage.

As you read *Faith Fitness,* continue to reflect upon the spiritual condition of your church. Feel free to refine any thoughts that have been prompted thus far. Becoming a fit church depends upon your prayerful reflection on the condition of your church and the condition of your heart as a leader.

1. List your church's strengths and weaknesses. Create one composite list.

2. Share with the group a list of your good memories at the church. How does your list overlap with the lists of other leaders? Discuss the personal nature of each leader's list.

3. Each leader should share his or her list of bad or traumatic memories with the group. Explain why each memory is bad or traumatic. Discuss. List the church memories that were in common among the leadership.

4. Bad memories or behaviors can represent scars on your church. What have been the consequences of those behaviors? Make a list of people who may have been offended or treated unfairly. Do any memories represent events or behaviors that have had a lasting impact on your church? Discuss.

5. Each leader should share their thoughts on the future of the church. Make a list.

Understanding Fitness: Definitions Ruach

Organizationally, it is important to have a common definition for terms like "health," "wellness," and "fitness." Leaders need a construct with which to evaluate their members and themselves. Recently, I went to a big box supply store for building supplies. I happened to walk in with a person who had just emerged from their car parked in a handicap space. I slowed my pace to match the infirmed gentleman and asked, "How's your health?"

The man said, "Great!"

"Really?" I asked. I told him that I noticed he was using a cane.

The floodgates then opened. The man told me he had metabolic syndrome (obesity, hypertension, diabetes, and hypercholesterolemia), gout, and congestive heart failure. He said that he was miserable most of the day.

I told him that I was sorry for his discomfort, but I challenged him by asking why he originally answered that his health was "great."

He replied, "My health *is* great. I can do most of what I want to."

If the perception of our own health is skewed, can we honestly take charge of our wellness? Medical studies show that most individuals are poor representatives of judging the health condition of their bodies. Denial is a strong force. Likewise, church leaders may have a bias about their own ekklesia. I would take this concept one step further by saying that leadership in most ekklesias give an inaccurate assessment of their spiritual condition. Sometimes we need guidance. Hayward's model of enthusiasm and recovery curves, the member enthusiasm model, and Dale's Health Cycle each help leadership understand a different aspect of church fitness.

1. Discuss the differences between health, wellness, fitness, and optimal fitness.

2. Why is the concept of a fit culture necessary for churches? Describe the importance of optimal fitness in your church.

3. Where is your church on Hayward's graph? Looking over the past five years, is your church moving downward or upward? Do you agree with his definition of enthusiasm? Explain. How is it similar and different than being in-dwelt by the Holy Spirit?

4. Where is your church presently on Robert Dale's Health Cycle? Has leadership recently discussed new goals, vision, or processes to better accomplish the will of God for your ekklesia?

5. The Fitness Corollary compares a church to the human body. Review and discuss the comparisons for health, wellness, fitness, and optimal fitness.

Understanding Fitness: Disease Ruach

In this chapter, we come face-to-face with diseases within our churches. We are not infectious disease experts, but we can recognize infirmity and afflictions among us without a CSI-type investigation. Your church may have any combination of asynchronous, swollen, dilated, thickened, or hardened heart(s) as described in the clinical archetypes of the Revelation churches that Jesus criticized. Only consultation with the Great Physician can help reveal the condition of your own church's heart.

To be a fit body of Christ, we must be functional and present with him. Leadership must control internal and external forces that could limit, harm, or weaken our church. Churches must develop a fit archetype so our spiritual muscles can serve the Lord despite our limitations. By being true to the Word of God and surrendering wholly to Christ, the church body might come to know the will of God for their ekklesia. Fit churches share the gospel with the next generation. The assignment for church leadership is to build an organization that can accomplish the ingredients of a fit Body and live a fitness lifestyle. The hallmark of a wellness-oriented church is that leadership manages disease and conflict and keeps the church focused on its vision, mission, and purpose.

1. Review the table of the unhealthy church archetypes. Do you see any of these traits in your church now? What were/are the contributing factors? Explain.

2. List internal and external obstacles that you and your leadership face in your church.

3. Based upon our definition of disease, do you see disease within your church? Discuss.

4. What responsibility do you have as a participant or leader in preventing disease and contributing to a healthy church culture? How can your leadership improve in its responsibility of becoming wellness-oriented?

5. Meet with members of your church's leadership, and discuss the most significant diseases that may be limiting your church.

Rx: Repent Ruach

In each of the Revelation churches that Christ criticized, he offered repentance as the antidote for their afflictions. Each of these churches had a dysfunctional heart toward Jesus. His criticism of their dysfunctional ekklesia was different for each church; nevertheless, the antidote was the same: repentance. Make notes of any sin, selfish behavior, or stressors that may be limiting you or your ekklesia.

Too often a church attempts to ride out its illness only to find it has metastasis out of neglect. A sick patient who receives an accurate diagnosis can be both troubled and relieved. The problem is documented—and must be treated. There can be no denial.

Perfect peace comes with truth. Repentance is the cure. After repentance, the Body can look forward to the future and better times. The process grows dependence on the Lord and faith. First, we must recognize our infirmities. Then, we must recognize that our healing comes only from the Great Physician!

Understanding how God and church visitors see our church may help us recognize our dysfunctional heart and lead us toward a journey of holiness. The English word "holy" is derived from the Anglo-Saxon *halig*; *hal* means "well" or "whole." The cure for a dysfunctional heart begins with repentance. If we repent as leaders, as a leadership body, and as a church, then we are worthy of Jesus saying to us as he said to the lame man, "'Get up! Pick up your mat and walk.' At once the man was cured; he picked up his mat and walked."[8]

1. Review the following list of church behaviors considered corporate sins. Circle the sins that you believe to be in your church. Can you list any other corporate sins?

Arrogance	Dead or incomplete works	Lack of evangelism
Apathy	False teaching	Materialism
Allowing status quo	Forsaking first love	Self-pride
Complacency	Faithless	Unacceptable behaviors
Critical spirit	Gossiping	Unwilling leadership
Others	_____	_____

2. Do some members of your church harbor any residual animosity over past conflicts or memories listed during the previous ruachs? How does a church body get beyond the past?

3. Make a list of the corporate sins committed by your church in one column. In the adjacent, corresponding column, create a statement that renounces that sin. Consider the following examples: Complacency—We renounce complacency and pledge to be a faithful community who serves the living Christ according to our vision, mission, purpose, and focus. Lack of Evangelism—We renounce that evangelism has not been an important part of our church, and we announce our commitment to bring the gospel of Jesus Christ to our neighbors in the world.

4. Individually and as a leadership group, confess and repent of the church's bad behaviors and corporate sins. Meet with ordained leadership, and consider a church service in which the congregation may participate in a service of repentance. Include the document that renounces corporate sins.

5. As a leader in your church, have you committed any of the sins mentioned in *Faith Fitness* by Patricia St. John in her book *Missing the Way*? If so, confess and repent of them privately and/or publicly as you are led. If you have been hurt by anyone in your church, forgive them. Have you been involved in any relationship that requires reconciliation?

Fitness Toolbox Ruach

The fitness toolbox was created from a fitness model that uses three different perspectives: biblical metaphors of the church, ordained clergy who have written books on church health, and academic studies that are published in peer-reviewed journals. The toolbox has many different types of tools that can be used to improve church health. Leaders need to develop skill in using the tools so their churches can be renewed organizationally. By focusing on factors that have actually been shown to be drivers for health, common mistakes can be avoided.

Biblical metaphors of the Church give clinical insight into the ingredients of fit New Testament churches. The bride metaphor teaches vision and purpose, the branch metaphor teaches focus and passion, and the body metaphor teaches the mission of churches. Altogether they example the most important driver discovered within the categorical analysis from theologians: the Mind of Christ. Do not underestimate the importance of developing the Mind of Christ in your church. The remainder of the church drivers are listed in order of importance and priority. Strategies to develop leadership, evangelism, discipleship, worship, and the presence of the Holy Spirit should be emphasized.

Academic factors that have been tested in the crucible of church life are also important tools available to leaders. By developing the Mind of Christ for your church, leaders are giving the membership purpose and direction. Leaders can flesh out a strategy for each church driver by listing the academic factors under the church areas of context, program, process, and identity that may help accomplish your goals. Using the toolbox to develop strategies builds enthusiasm among members and springboards the church to a wellness orientation.

1. Review the chart of "A Fit Ekklesia" and review the ingredients of a healthy church culture. The biblical metaphors also serve as a template for the Mind of Christ. Meet with other leaders from your church and encourage your entire leadership to take the *Faith Fitness* journey. Begin creating a vision,

purpose, focus, and mission for your church. Share with your clergy and leadership group.

2. What is meant by the word "driver" in the context of the Fitness Toolbox? What is a categorical analysis? Why is it useful for organizations?

3. Discuss the ranking order within the categorical analysis. Would you have ranked the categories differently? Break into groups and rank the same drivers into an order that your church needs to address as contributing to its health. Which driver could you build your mission around or could accomplish the mission created above?

4. Review the academic factors listed in the table Academic Factors with Church Drivers. Select one church driver from the list that your church needs to address (e.g., evangelism). Using the academic factors associated with growth that are listed next to that driver, make a rank order list of the factors that could be incorporated into your church. Can you think of any additional factors (not found among the academic factors) that would support your list?

5. From the rank order list of the previous question, choose one factor and flesh out a strategy to make that a reality in your church. Brainstorm and

discuss the various programs that would help to develop, support, and enhance the selected factor. Congratulations, you are using the wellness toolbox!

Rx: Renew and Recommit Ruach

As a leadership group, we have confessed, repented, and renounced certain sins and behaviors. The process frees our church from the bondage of sin, prepares the church for a season of renewal and recommitment, and elevates the ekklesia to a wellness orientation. When we restore Jesus to the headship of our church, renewal is possible. Church renewal grows from the remnant of dedicated and faithful servants within every ekklesia. Even the Revelation churches that Jesus criticized had a remnant of faithful followers that were commended. Joshua gathered the faithful leaders from the tribes of Israel to create a covenant renewal with God.[9] Renewal for your church begins with the repentant hearts of faithful leaders, too.

The apostle Peter recommitted his life to Christ on the shore of the Sea of Galilee.[10] Paul committed his life to Christ when he regained his sight in the house of Judas on Straight Street.[11] The disciples recommitted their lives to Christ after his resurrection, before he ascended near the Mt. of Olives.[12] There have been times in my life when recommitment was necessary. During my thirty-three years of practicing newborn intensive care medicine, I have at times, recommitted myself to serving others (above myself and my family), despite the difficult hours and emotional toll. Every time that we relocated during training, my wife and I recommitted to serving the Lord in a new church. When leadership commits to Christ, blessings follow.

1. Discuss how you feel after participating in the previous exercise, Repentance Ruach. Which steps were difficult for you? Do you or your leadership have any unfinished business before claiming renewal?

2. When was the last time that your leadership approached God for a season of renewal? Describe the occasion.

3. What kind of person or leader would stand in the way of their church taking steps to improve their level of fitness? Should we put them out like Jesus did in Mathew 9:25? How do we handle this difficult situation in our church?

4. As a group, write a prayer of renewal. Allow it to be a covenant between you and God and between your leadership and his church. Share it with the ordained and non-ordained leadership. Allow input for final revisions. Consider incorporating the prayer into a service of renewal before the church congregation.

5. Recommitment to Christ is a natural step after repentance and renewal. Read John 21, the story of Peter being restored as a disciple. Have group members share their church leadership position(s) with the others. Consider

making a statement that expresses your commitment to Christ, the Church, and your church.

Fit Body Ruach

This chapter began by sharing a CrossFit experience between two guys who like to work out. The sessions are created to be relationally interconnected. The atmosphere is one of a community who shares dietary regimens and lifestyle choices that help them get in better physical shape. The Peloton® company sells a sedentary bike with an online streaming experience that also offers a relational community atmosphere. These examples are provided to help church leaders understand how the next generation, Millennials, like to function. Just like people, churches have a Body that needs to be in shape. The major drivers for church health were compared to the human body.

Jesus is the head of the church Body. Ordained and lay leadership have a co-leader symbiosis in communicating the Mind of Christ to congregants. Leaders should use appropriate techniques if they want to properly communicate to every generation, especially the Millennial generation. Lay leadership may be the heart of the Body, but the Holy Spirit gives the Church and every church its functional heartbeat. Muscles are useless unless they are fit to serve the Body. Spiritual training of the muscles (followers) allows the vision and purpose of the church to be fulfilled. Evangelism is the fullest expression of a fit church. Passing the ecclesial DNA of the gospel to the next generation of believers fulfills the definition of fitness, is the integral ingredient of a fit church archetype (soul-winning and succession-minded), and completes the vision and purpose of the Body metaphor.

1. Discuss the CrossFit philosophy of fitness. How is it different from your workout experience? The younger generations require a different culture and experience. How can their needs be incorporated into our churches?

2. How is a church Body like a human body? How is it different? Explain how the church-body comparison helps us understand our leadership roles and responsibilities in making our church Body fit.

3. Is the Holy Spirit truly the heartbeat of the Church and our churches? List the ways your church may be quenching and igniting the presence of the Holy Spirit. Discuss.

4. Do you agree with the statement that lay leadership or non-ordained church leaders should be co-leaders with the ordained leadership? Why? Discuss the roles and balance of each in your faith tribe.

5. Evangelism is one of the most important drivers of church health. Review the data of U.S. church attendance as well as that of your own church. How well is your church doing? Does it need to improve? Is this an area that your leadership should focus upon? Discuss.

Rx: Respond Ruach

As a leader, the prescription to respond is a challenge. The heart of your ekklesia is healthier because you better understand the healthy church archetype and the afflictions of poor organizational structures. Improving the level of fitness within your church is a goal worth achieving. Creating a fit Body and a healthy culture is essential to developing a fitness lifestyle. Some of you are solitary travelers from your churches. Others are taking this journey in groups. Every reader should benefit from this fitness journey, but each leader may have a different response.

Ascending the mountain of change required of ordained and non-ordained leaders in today's church landscape is now possible. Not every church will summit the fitness spectrum, but every church leader can respond to the fitness challenge.

1.   Describe how *Faith Fitness* has helped your own spiritual fitness. Which exercise has been the most meaningful to you? Why?

2.   Go to the faithfitnessmovement.com website. Review the contents and resources available to you and your church leadership.

3.   For solitary travelers, share this information and your *Faith Fitness* experience with your clergy and other lay leaders at your church. Begin with informal meetings. Encourage them to read *Faith Fitness* as a group. Allow congregants who are not leaders to participate, especially younger members. Order one of the books listed in the resources section. Determine the best meeting time for the group to discuss each chapter and complete the Ruach exercises. Consider leading the group.

4. For small teams of travelers, meet with your clergy and the entire church leadership. Encourage them to take the *Faith Fitness* journey together.

5. Describe the obstacles to getting full participation from leaders in your church. How might you overcome these obstacles? Sometimes our time is not God's time. Pray that God would prepare the hearts of your leadership for a season of health and fitness.

Fitness Lifestyle Ruach

This final chapter helps leaders understand their role in the fitness center, but, more importantly, it demonstrates the life of individual believers who are growing and maturing in churches. The transformative process that is called T⁵ creates a church culture whose goal is to transform believers into fit followers by having them work out together systematically.

T⁵ has at least five spiritual stations that can engage members to train in a variety of ways. Some exercises are performed within the facility. Other training opportunities are done outside the church. Trainees should be allowed to participate either physically or virtually. Being in community helps to create the fitness lifestyle. Doing with community teaches followers how to overcome trials and temptations. Trainers serve as mentors who help build knowledge, skill, and Christian maturity in a creative atmosphere.

The Scripture that best exemplifies the T⁵ culture is found in Romans 12. In verse one, Paul begins by saying, "Therefore, I urge you, brothers and sisters, in view of God's mercy, to offer your bodies as a living sacrifice, holy and pleasing to God—this is your true and proper worship." He talks of being transformed by the renewing of our minds. Every follower is needed for different types of service and for the health of the body. Each of us should live in harmony with one another and be devoted to one another in brotherly love. T⁵ builds bonds and creates teamwork among believers in training, which is a winning formula for the Millennial generation.

After the Body has developed fit followers, they are sent out to share the heart and love of Christ with the world. These worthy followers now "run the race" for their Savior. *Doing* with community really means reproducing followers (enthusiasts) who are committed to the mission of the church. *Doing* demonstrates that "faith without works is dead" [13] and "faith... worketh by love." [14] By actively participating in their ekklesia's mission, followers are creating an enthusiasm for carrying out Christ's vision locally within community and at a distance in the world as a Body.

1. Describe the church's role in creating a spiritual fitness center. Explain the most difficult part of creating a fitness lifestyle within your church.

2. The T⁵ diagram can be viewed on the left side as "Doing" and on the right side as "Being." Describe the difference. How might one affect the other in discipleship and maturity?

3. Describe each T⁵ fitness station from the perspective of the church (together, table, teach, train, and touch) and of the trainee (together, sit, study, serve, and share). Describe the needs of believers from different generations.

4. Develop one T⁵ program for a younger generation and another for an older generation. Include the wisdom of people (and clergy) from each generation. Take a trainee through the five fitness stations of your newly developed T⁵ training center, and discuss how each station contributes to building up a fit follower.

5. Describe the gifts, skill, and training for an effective T⁵ trainer. How can your church develop trainers to mentor young believers?

Rx: Run the Race

Comparing athletes in training with believers in spiritual training is appropriate. The apostle Paul used that analogy in 1 Timothy 4:8 when he said, "For physical training is of some value, but godliness has value for all things, holding promise for both the present life and the life to come." The key to an intimate relationship with Jesus Christ, however, is following daily habits that become a lifestyle routine. The spiritual disciplines of Scripture reading, prayer, and fellowship are examples of habits that take place privately and corporately within the Church.

When believers train and run the race despite adversity, limitations, or excuses, God can touch others with the love of Christ and the light of the gospel. When the Body works the heart of Christ into her neighbors, the ekklesia wins, for God is longing to reveal himself to those in affliction. Building faith is the key to believer commitment, transformation, and discipleship. Without faith, the use of God's Church is limited. Without faith, we never experience the fullness of the fitness lifestyle—joy, peace, and contentment.

1. With the help of these exercises, you are well on your way to elevating the fitness level of your church. Finally, have your leadership decide on a fitness goal for your church, such as the level of fitness you want to achieve. Meet to review and mark the necessary steps that will help to accomplish this organizational goal and culture.

2. Develop the Mind of Christ for your church, if you haven't already done so. Use the fit Body analogy to communicate it to the Body and build enthusiasm.

3. Determine the generation or group of people you want to serve and bring the gospel to in your community. Use the wellness toolbox to build an evangelism strategy. Discuss the church structure and processes that will be necessary to accomplish your mission.

4. Build the structure, processes, and ministries to support your mission. Encourage church-wide participation, for every spiritual gift will be useful. Discuss the accountability that will be necessary to maintain the fitness culture.

5. Create a spiritual fitness center within your church to disciple and mature the new attendees. Select the trainers that will work with believers. Thoughtfully develop the five T^5 training stations that will mature believers into fit followers. A few churches are ready to build or plant a new ekklesia. Study the different models and discuss. Embark on a quest to accomplish this important task in the Kingdom.

Endnotes

Preface

1   Corinthians 11:28

Introduction

1   Mark 2:21-22

2   The Physician's Executive MBA, PEMBA, was earned thru the collaboration of the Southern Medical Society and Auburn University in 2003. Sharp received the STAR award from Pediatrix Medical Group for excellence in medical practice in 2004. A traditional MBA was earned from Brenau University in 2009.

3   Metcalfe, Simon and Sharp, Cecil, "Enthusiasm and Congregational Growth: Evidence from the United Methodist Church," *International Journal of Business and Social Science*, Vol. 3 No.9; May 2012.

4   Olson, David T., *The American Church in Crisis*, (Zondervan, 2008).

Chapter 1: The Journey

1   *Everest Rescue* TV Mini Series. accessed January 2, 2018, www.imdb.com/title/tt6403100/.

2   Ed Viesturs keynote speaker on Teamwork at Mednax National Medical Directors meeting, Orlando, Florida, April 22, 2012.

3   Isaiah 40:4

4   *Ekklesia* is the Greek form used in New Testament writings for a body of faithful people and is used in this book. The Latin form *ecclesia* is also sometimes used.

5   Exodus 33:7-20

6   Prince, Derek, *God's Medicine Bottle*, (New Kensingston, Pennsylvania: Derek Prince Ministries, Whitaker House, 1984).

7   Proverbs 4:20-23

8   Exodus 15:25

9   Leviticus 10:1-2

10 John 21:1-12

11 Prince, Derek, *God's Medicine Bottle*, (New Kensingston, Pennsylvania: Derek Prince Ministries, Whitaker House, 1984), 36.6

12 Exodus 13:21

13 Matthew 13:44

14 Quote by Henri Nouwen, *Making All Things New,* from *A Guide to Prayer for Ministers and other Servants*, by R. P. Job and N. Shawchuck (Nashville, Tennessee: The Upper Room).

15 John 8:47

16 Buford, Bob, *Halftime: Moving from Success to Significance*, (Grand Rapids, Michigan: Zondervan, 1994).

17 Matthew 14:23

18 Mark 6:31

19 Jeremiah 6:16

20 Exodus 33

21 Psalm 73:26

22 John 4:13

23 John 7:37

24 Isaiah 30:21

Chapter 2: Church Culture

1   Culture. Merriam-Webster Dictionary. Accessed May 6, 2018, from Merriam-Webster.com website: https://www.merriam-webster.com/dictionary/culture.

2 Neil Patel Blog at NeilPatel.com, accessed May 18, 2019, from https://neilpatel.com/blog/googles-culture-of-success/.

3 McGee, J. Vernon, *Thru the Bible with J. Vernon McGee: Volume V, 1 Corinthians–Revelation*, (Nashville, Tennessee: Thomas Nelson Publishers, 1983), 898-899.

4 Romans 7:24 NET

5 Revelation 2:1-7

6 Revelation 2:2

7 Revelation 2:4

8 Hebrews 13:5

9 Revelation 2:5

10 Revelation 2:12-17

11 Revelation 2:13

12 1 Timothy 6:3-5

13 1 Corinthians 1:20

14 1 Corinthians 1:19

15 Revelation 2:18-29

16 Acts 16:14

17 Revelation 2:19

18 Revelation 2:20-22

19 Tozer A. W., *The Counselor: Straight Talk About the Holy Spirit*, (Camp hill, Pennsylvania: Wing Spread Publishers, 2009), 121.

20 Revelation 3:1-6

21 Revelation 3:1-2

22 Revelation 3:14-22

23 Colossians 1:7, 4:12-13

24 Revelation 3:15-17

25 1 Timothy 6:17-19

26 Tozer A. W., *The Warfare of the Spirit*, (Camp Hill, Pennsylvania: Widespread Publishers, 2006), 10-11.

27 Psalm 22:14

28 Ezekiel 36:26

29 Revelation 3:8-10

30 Revelation 2:9 KJV

31 McGee J. V., *Thru the Bible with J. Vernon McGee, volume V:1 Corinthians–Revelation*, (Nashville, Tennessee: Thomas Nelson Publishers, 1983), 904-906 and 915-920.

32 Sigler, T.M., "Reading Revelation 2-3 As If You Were There," *Messianic Perspectives*, Lyyar-Sivan-Tammuz, 5770/May-June 2010, pages 1-7.

33 McGee J. V., *Thru the Bible with J. Vernon McGee, volume V:1 Corinthians–Revelation*, (Nashville, Tennessee: Thomas Nelson Publishers, 1983), 904-906 and 915-920.

34 Revelation 3:8,10

35 Ephesians 2:8-10

36 James 2:18

37 McGee J. V., (1983). *Thru the Bible with J. Vernon McGee, volume V:1 Corinthians–Revelation*, (Nashville, Tennessee: Thomas Nelson Publishers, 1983), 904-906 and 915-920.

38 Romans 12:3

39 Acts 1:7-8; Romans 8:25

40 Philippians 2:10

41 1 Thessalonians 1:5

42 2 Corinthians 8:1-5

43 1 Thessalonians 3:6-7

44 McGee J. V., (1983). *Thru the Bible with J. Vernon McGee, volume V:1 Corinthians–Revelation*, (Nashville, Tennessee: Thomas Nelson Publishers, 1983), 368.

45 Hebrews 12:1

46 Ephesians 4:1

47 Philippians 1:27

48 Colossians 1:10, 1 Thessalonians 2:12, 3 John 6

49 Revelations 2:8-11 and 3:7-13

50 Medcalfe, Simon and Sharp, Cecil, "Enthusiasm and Congregational Growth: Evidence from the United Methodist Church," *International Journal of Business and Social Science*, Vol. 3 No.9; May 2012.

51 Oxford Dictionary-Definition of nominal in English, accessed October 2, 2017, https://en.oxforddictionaries.com/definition/nominal.

52 Philippians 3:18-19

53 Philippians 3:13-16

54 Colossians 2:6-7

55 1 Chronicles 16:29 KJV

56 Psalm 78

57 1 Thessalonians 2:19

58 Paraphrased from Philippians 1:21-22

59 Psalm 139:23-24

60 Amos 7:8

61 Ephesians 4:18

62 John 5:1-8

63 Jeremiah 2:13

64 Sweet, Leonard,. *I Am a Follower: The Way, Truth, and Life of Following Jesus.* (Nashville, Tennessee: Thomas Nelson, 2012).

65 1 Kings 19:11-12

Chapter 3: Understanding Fitness

1 President's Physical Fitness Award. Wikipedia free dictionary. Accessed January 3, 2018 from Wikipedia.org website: https://en.wikipedia.org/wiki/President%27s_Council_on_Fitness,_Sports,_and_Nutrition http://en.wikipedia.org/wiki/President's_Council_on_Fitness,_Sports,_and_Nutrition

2 Campbell, Adam, "A Fit Man Can," *Men's Health*, January 2011, 8-17.

3 Luke 6:48

4 1 Samuel 17:42

5 health. (n.d.). *Dictionary.com Unabridged.* Accessed December 12, 2017, from Dictionary.com website: http://www.dictionary.com/browse/health.

6 Health–"a state of complete physical, mental and social well-being and not merely the absence of disease," WHO 1974 soundness of body and mind; vigor, vitality, strength or stamina. Accessed December 12, 2017, https://www.dictionary.com/browse/health.

7 health. (n.d.). *Merriam-Webster's Medical Dictionary.* Accessed December 12, 2017, From Dictionary.com website: http://dictionary.reference.com/browse/health.

8 Day, William Jr., "The Development of a Comprehensive Definition of Church Health," presented at the Ola Farmer Lenaz Lecture submitted to the faculty of the New Orleans Baptist Theological Seminary, on December 19, 2002.

9 Matthew 28:16-20

10 Matthew 22:36-37

11 wellness. (n.d.). *The American Heritage® Stedman's Medical Dictionary,* accessed December 12, 2017, from Dictionary.com website: http://dictionary.reference.com/browse/wellness.

12 wellness. (n.d.). *Dictionary.com Unabridged,* accessed December 12, 2017, from Dictionary.com website: http://dictionary.reference.com/browse/wellness.

13 fitness. (n.d.). *The American Heritage® Stedman's Medical Dictionary,* accessed December 12, 2017, from Dictionary.com website: http://dictionary.reference.com/browse/fitness.

14 fitness. (n.d.). *Merriam-Webster's Medical Dictionary,* accessed December 12, 2017, from Dictionary.com website: http://dictionary.reference.com/browse/fitness.

15 Sweet, L., *11 Gateways to Spiritual Awakening*, (Nashville, Tennessee: Abingdon Press, 1998).

16 Marty, Martin E., "Never the Same Again: Post-Vatican II Catholic-Protestant Interactions. The Metaphor of Moraine and a New Social Contract," *Sociologic analysis*, Vol:52, issue:1, 1991, page 20.

17 Sweet, L., *11 Gateways to Spiritual Awakening*, (Nashville, Tennessee: Abingdon Press, 1998).

18 Luke 19.4

19 John 5

20 Hayward, John, "A General Model of Church Growth and Decline," *Journal of Mathematical Sociology*, 29, 2005, 177-207.

21 Hayward, John, "A General Model of Church Growth and Decline," *Journal of Mathematical Sociology*, 29, 2005, 177-207.

22 Viola, Frank, *Finding Organic Church*. (Colorado Springs, Colorado: David C. Cook, 2009), 261.

23 Kinnaman, David and Lyons, Gabe, *unChristian*, (Grand Rapids, Michigan: Baker Books, 2007).

24 Zaleski, Peter and Zech, Charles, "The Optimal Size of a Religious Congregation: An Economic Theory of Clubs Analysis," *The American Journal of Economics and Sociology*, 1995, 54:439-453.

25 Iannaccone, L.R., Olson, D.V.A., and Stark, R., "Religious resources and church Growth," *Social Forces*, 1995, 74(2), 705-731.

26 Hayward, John, "A General Model of Church Growth and Decline," *Journal of Mathematical Sociology*, 29, 2005, 177-207, pp. 181-183.

27 Hayward, John, "A General Model of Church Growth and Decline," *Journal of Mathematical Sociology*, 29, 2005, 177-207, p. 197. 7

28 Hayward, John, "A General Model of Church Growth and Decline," *Journal of Mathematical Sociology*, 29, 2005, 177-207..

29 Roozen, D.A., *Oldline Protestantism: pockets of vitality within a continuing stream of decline* (Hartford, CT, Hartford Institute for Religion research,

2004), accessed November 2010 at: http://hirr.hartsem.edu/bookshelf/roozen_article5.html.

30 Medcalfe and Sharp, "Enthusiasm and Congregational Growth: Evidence from the United Methodist Church," *International Journal of Business and Social Science*, Vol. 3 No.9; May 2012, p. 32.

31 1 John 4:13

32 Ezekiel 11:19

33 Colossians 3:12-14

34 Medcalfe and Sharp, "Enthusiasm and Congregational Growth: Evidence from the United Methodist Church," *International Journal of Business and Social Science*, Vol. 3 No.9; May 2012, pp. 33-34.

35 Warren, Rick, *The Purpose Driven Church*, (Grand Rapids, Michigan: Zondervan, 1995).

36 Dale, Robert D., *To Dream Again: How to Help Your Church Come Alive*, (Eugene, Oregon: Wipf & Stock Publishers, 2004), originally published by Broadman Press, 1981.

37 Dale, Robert D., *To Dream Again: How to Help Your Church Come Alive*, (Eugene, Oregon: Wipf & Stock Publishers, 2004), originally published by Broadman Press, 1981, 139.

38 WLPE 91.7 FM radio station, Augusta, Georgia. Research at http://www.joniandfriends.org, http://www.joniandfriends.org/?gclid=CjwKCAiAy4bTBRAvEiwAFtatHJclmNqNvWC-UYT5bR8K2HMnKRH_8KL6AEWvoSfIszKtRbIy8puxLBoCR4IQAvD_BwE

39 Revelation 2:8-11

40 Revelation 3:7-13

41 Kirkman, Robert, Moore, Tony, Adlard, Charlie. (Directors/Writers). (2011). AMC Television series. Mazzara, G., Durabont, F., Kirkmand R. (Executive Producers). *The Walking Dead*, accessed October 17, 2017 from: http://www.amctv.com/shows/the-walking-dead.

42 Revelation 3:1

43 disease. (n.d.). Merriam-Webster's Medical Dictionary, accessed October 17, 2017, from Dictionary.com website: http://dictionary.reference.com/browse/disease.

44 Romans 7:14-25

45 Hamel, Gary, "The 15 Diseases of Leadership, According to Pope Francis," *Harvard Business Review*, April 14, 2015.

46 St. John, Patricia, *Missing the Way*, (LaVergne, Tennessee: Harvey Christian Publishers Inc., Lightning Source, 2017).

47 Psalm 78:33 NKJV

48 McClatchy Newspapers, "Higher obesity rate found in clergy," *The Augusta Chronicle*, May 18, 2010, Section D, page 1.

49 1 Kings 19:9, 13

50 Roozen, David A., "American Congregations 2008: FACT—Faith Communities Today," Hartford Seminary, Hartford Institute for Religious Research, Hartford, CT, 2009, 1-37.

51 1 Peter 1:12

52 James 4:1

53 James 4:4-5

54 1 Corinthians 1:10

55 Roozen, pp. 26-27.

56 John 4:23-24 KJV

57 Romans 12:1

58 Roozen, pp. 5-9.

59 De Wetter, C., Gochman, I., Luss, R., and Sherwood, R., "A Call to Action: Vital Congregations Research Project," Towers Watson, pp. 5-9.

60 Roozen,) "American Congregations 2008: FACT—Faith Communities Today," Hartford Seminary, Hartford Institute for Religious Research, Hartford, CT, pp. 28-29.

61 Roozen, "American Congregations 2008: FACT—Faith Communities Today," Hartford Seminary, Hartford Institute for Religious Research, Hartford, CT. pp. 28-29.

62 James 1:2-12

63 C. S. Lewis, "Membership" in *The Weight of Glory: And Other Addresses* (New York: HarperCollins, 1949/2001), 171.

64 Malachi 1:6

65 Malachi 2:10-16

66 Malachi 3:7-12

67 Malachi 3:5

68 See the books of Habakkuk, Zechariah, and Malachi.

69 Acts 2:38

70 Matthew 3:2

71 Acts 20:21

72 Jonah 3:5-10

73 Matthew 3:2

74 Acts 26:20

75 https://www.merriam-webster.com/dictionary/repent

76 Thayer and Smith, "Greek Lexicon entry for Metanoeo," "The New Testament Greek… Lexicon," taken from http://www.searchgodsword.org/lex/grk/view.cgi?number=3340, accessed on February 1, 2012.

77 Bailey, A. M. and Tozer, A. W. (1897-1963), *Man the Dwelling Place of God: True Religion is not Feeling but Willing*, (The Alliance Witness), 34.

78 Acts 3:19

79 Luke 23:34

80 2 Chronicles 7:14

81 Luke 15:11-32

82 Ezekiel 11:19

83 Isaiah 43:25

Chapter 4: Fitness Toolbox

1 1 Corinthians 12:12-27

2 1 Corinthians 12:25

3 Ephesians 4:1-6 and Colossians 2:19

4 Ephesians 4:6

5 Tozer, *The Pursuit of God*, (Christian Publications, 1993), 156-157.

6 Ephesians 1:22-23

7 John 3:29

8 2 Corinthians 11:2

9 Ephesians 5:23

10 Matthew 17:5

11 1 Corinthians 6:17 BSB

12 Luke 3:8-9

13 Mark 11:12-21

14 Job, Rueben P. and Shawchuck, Norman. *A Guide to Prayer*, (Nashville, Tennessee: The Upper Room, 1983), 203-204. Taken from *Spirituality for Ministry* by Urban T. Holmes.

15 Job, Rueben P. and Shawchuck, Norman. *A Guide to Prayer*, (Nashville, Tennessee: The Upper Room, 1983), 320. Taken from *The Spiritual Life* by Evelyn Underhill.

16 Colossians 1:18

17 Colossians 2:19

18 1 Corinthians 3:6

19 Zaleski, Peter and Zech, Charles, "The Optimal Size of a Religious congregation: An Economic Theory of Clubs Analysis," *The American Journal of Economics and Sociology*, 1995, 54:439-453.

20 Medcalfe and Sharp, "Enthusiasm and Congregational Growth," *The International Journal of Business and Social Science*, vol.3 no.9, 2012, p. 39.

21 Finck, R. and Stark, R., "The churching of America, 1776-1990: Winners and losers in America's religious economy," (Rutgers University Press, 1992).

22 Zaleski and Zech.

23 Medcalfe and Sharp, "Enthusiasm and Congregational Growth," *The International Journal of Business and Social Science*, vol.3 no.9, 2012, p. 30-39.

24 Hayward, John, "A General Model of Church Growth and Decline," *Journal of Mathematical Sociology*, 2005, 29, 177-207.

25 Perrin, R. D., Kennedy, P., and Miller, D.E. "Examining sources of conservative church growth: Where are the new evangelical movements getting their numbers?", *Journal for the Scientific Study of Religion*, 1997, 36(1):71-80.

26 Iannaccone, Laurence R., Olson, Daniel V.A., Stark, Rodney. "Religious Resources and Church Growth," *Social Forces,* 1995, vol. 74, issue 2, p. 705.

27 Zaleski, Peter, and Zech, Charles. "The Optimal Size of a Religious congregation: An Economic Theory of Clubs Analysis," *The American Journal of Economics and Sociology*, 1995, 54:439-453.

28 Weems, Lovett H., Jr., Arnold, Joseph E., and Michel, Ann A., "A Lewis Center Report: Clergy Age Trends in the United Methodist Church 1985-2009," Wesley Theological Seminary, Lewis Center for Church Leadership, p. 1-6, accessed March 20, 2010: http://www.churchleadership.com/research/um_clergy_age_trends09.htm.

29 *The Augusta Chronicle*, August 20, 2011, "Study Shows fewer women in the pews: 20-year research's findings not surprise, some clergy say," Barna.

30 1 Kings 8:51

31 Ezra 1-6

32 Ezra 10:1-4 and Nehemiah 10:28-29

33 Romans 12:2

34 Joshua 24:1-28

35 Joshua 24:14-15 ESV

36 Matthew 22:35-37

37 John 21:15, 19

38 Colossians 2:19

39 Ephesians 4:4-5

40 Quote by Soren Kierkegaard, *The Prayers of Kierkegaard,* from *A Guide to Prayer* by R. P. Job and N. Shawchuck, (Nashville, Tennessee: The Upper Room, 1983), 211.

41 1 Peter 1:3

42 Deuteronomy 6:4-9

43 Mark 12:29-30

44 1 Peter 2:9

45 Luke 13:6-9

46 James 4:4 KJV

47 1 John 2:15 KJV

48 John 21:1-5

49 Luke 5:6

50 John 21:15-19

51 Philippians 1:22

52 John 3:6

53 Romans 8:5-6

54 Colossians 3:1-17

Chapter 5: Fit Body

1 Cej, Marty, *The Business of Crossfit,* The Crossfit Journal Articles, 2009, 1-11.

2 1 Timothy 4:8

3 1 Timothy 4:7

4 1 Timothy 4:7-16, 1 Samuel 18-26, Colossians 3:23

5 Psalm 96:9 KJV

6 Psalm 78

7 1 Corinthians 6:20

8 Ephesians 4:1-6 and Colossians 2:19

9   Warren, Rick, *The Purpose Driven Church,* (Grand Rapids, Michigan: Zondervan, 1995), 107.

10 1 Corinthians 3:6

11 Matthew 22:37-40

12 Matthew 28:19-20

13 Matthew 9:37

14 Acts 6:1-7

15 McDonald's Ambition Statement, 2017, accessed January 10, 2018: http://corporate.mcdonalds.com/mcd/our_company/our-ambition.html

16 Acts 2:2

17 *NIV Study Bible,* (Grand Rapids, Michigan: Zondervan Publishing House, 1985), footnote to Ephesians 5:18, 1798.

18 Genesis 1:30

19 Jeremiah 38:16

20 Ezekiel 37:5

21 Zechariah 4:6

22 Ephesians 4:30

23 heart. (n.d.). Easton's 1897 Bible Dictionary, accessed October 28, 2017, from Dictionary.com website: http://dictionary.reference.com/browse/heart.

24 Deuteronomy 6:5 and 26:16, Matthew 22:37, Mark 12:30-33

25 Romans 2:15

26 1 Kings 3:12

27 Psalms 24:4, Matthew 5:8

28 Genesis 20:5-6, Psalms 11:2 and 78:72, 1 Kings 8:15

29 Genesis 8:21

30 Matthew 12:34 and 15:18, Ecclesiastes 8:11, Psalm 73:7

31 Philippians 1:22

32 Viola, Frank, *Finding Organic Church*, (Colorado Springs, Colorado: David C. Cook, 2009), 71.

33 Acts 2

34 John 15:16

35 John 16:13

36 Philippians 4:13

37 Ephesians 4:12

38 United Methodist Church news release to pastors, July 12, 2010, Nashville, Tennessee.

39 Medcalfe, Simon and Sharp, Cecil, "Enthusiasm and Congregational Growth: Evidence from the United Methodist Church," *International Journal of Business and Social Science*, Vol. 3 No.9; May 2012.

40 MacDonald, Jefferey G., "More young adults heeding pastoral call: Demographics and cultural forces cited," *USA Today*, 6D, page 1, August 9, 2010.

41 heart. (n.d.). Dictionary.com Unabridged, accessed October 28, 2017, from Dictionary.com website: http://dictionary.reference.com/browse/heart.

42 Psalm 4:7 footnote

43 Proverbs 4:23

44 1 Corinthians 12

45 Heenan, David A. and Bennis, Warren, *Business Leadership: The Case for Co-Leaders*, (San Francisco, California: Jossey-Bass A Wiley Imprint, 2003).

46 Romans 12:8

47 1 Corinthians 12:38

48 Acts 6:3

49 Acts 6:5

50 Acts 6:7

51 1 Timothy 3

52 1 Timothy 5 and Titus 1

53 Nouwen, Henri J.M., *In the Name of Jesus: Reflections on Christian Leadership*, (New York: The Crossroad Publishing Company, 2002), 38.

54 *The American Medical Association Encyclopedia of Medicine*, 703-706; Brandreth, Gyles, *Your Vital Statistics*, 17; Cody, John, *Visualizing Muscles*, 5.

55 1 Corinthians 12:12

56 1 Corinthians 12:12

57 1 Corinthians 12

58 Ephesians 4:1

59 Romans 6:4

60 Ephesians 2:10

61 Ephesians 5:2

62 Colossians 4:5

63 3 John 4

64 1 Thessalonians 4:10

65 MacLaren, Alexander, *Expositions of Holy Scripture*, accessed January 5, 2018, from http://biblehub.com/commentaries/maclaren/revelation/3.htm.

66 1 Timothy 5:22

67 1 Timothy 4:7

68 1 Thessalonians 5:19

69 1 Timothy 1:19, 1 Timothy 6:12

70 2 Timothy 2:3-7, Ephesians 6

71 1 Corinthians 9:24-27, Philippians 3:14, Mathew 25:21

72 1 Peter 1:23

73 1 Thessalonians 1:3

74 2 Thessalonians 2:15

75 1 Timothy 6:18

76 Revelation 3:4

77 Sweet, Leonard, *I Am a Follower: The Way, Truth and Life of Following Jesus*, (Nashville, Tennessee: Thomas Nelson, 2012), 9.

78 Sweet, Leonard, *I Am a Follower: The Way, Truth and Life of Following Jesus*, (Nashville, Tennessee: Thomas Nelson, 2012), 12.

79 Olson, David T., *The American Church in Crisis*, (Grand Rapids, Michigan: Zondervan, 2008), 120, 145-146.

80 Jeremiah 1:10

81 Olson, David T., *The American Church in Crisis*, (Grand Rapids, Michigan: Zondervan, 2008), 83.

82 Olson, David T., *The American Church in Crisis*, (Grand Rapids, Michigan: Zondervan, 2008), 125.

83 Olson, David T., *The American Church in Crisis*, (Grand Rapids, Michigan: Zondervan, 2008), 131-134.

84 Matthew 22:39

85 Matthew 28:19

86 Breckenridge, Mary Beth. "Dilapidated old church is now family's home," *The Augusta Chronicle*, Section E, Today's Home, October 23, 2011, 3.

87 McClatchy Newspapers, "Evangelists target New England," Associated Press, *The Augusta Chronicle*, November 14, 2009, 3D.

88 Olson, David T., *The American Church in Crisis*, (Grand Rapids, Michigan: Zondervan, 2008), 120-122.

89 Olson, David T., *The American Church in Crisis*, (Grand Rapids, Michigan: Zondervan, 2008), 149-150.

90 Viola, Frank, *Finding Organic Church: A Comprehensive Guide to Starting and Sustaining Authentic Christian Communities*, (Colorado Springs, Colorado: David C. Cook, 2009), 25-50.

91 Surratt, Geoff, Ligon, Greg, and Bird, Warren, *The Multi-site Church Revolution*, (Grand Rapids, Michigan: Zondervan, 2006).

92 Grossman, Cathy Lynn, "New face of evangelism: 1 church, multiple sites," *USA Today*, December 17, 2009, 1A page 1.

93 John 12:26

94 John 9:4

Chapter 6: Fitness Lifestyle

1 Galatians 2:2, 5:7 and Philippians 2:16

2 1 Timothy 6:12

3 Hebrews 12:1

4   Luke 2:49

5   Luke 2:46-47

6   John 4:34

7   Matthew 4:4

8   Hebrews 4:12

9   Acts 2:46-47

10 Acts 1:14

11 Acts 2:42

12 Acts 2:32

13 Luke 22:20

14 Matthew 6:5-13, Luke 11:1

15 Mark 11:24-25

16 John 17:20 – protect them from the evil one; Luke 19:46 – house of prayer; Mark 9:29 – some deliverance requires prayer

17 Acts 1:14

18 I John 1:8-9

19 1 Timothy 2:1

20 The Bible directs, "When you fast…," not *if* you fast. Many good books are written on this subject and should be reviewed before using this tool, especially for people with medical issues.

21 Genesis chapter 1, and 1:2 specifically.

22 John 1:32-34

23 John 7:3b-38 BSB

24 John 4:10, 14

25 Matthew 15:8-9

26 Hemphill, Ken, *The Antioch Effect: 8 Characteristics of Highly Effective Churches*, (Nashville, Tennessee: Broadman & Holman Publishers, 1994).

27 2 Timothy 2:2

28 Hemphill, Ken, *The Antioch Effect: 8 Characteristics of Highly Effective Churches*, (Nashville, Tennessee, 1994), 181-204.

29 John 10:7, 11

30 John 21:15-17

31 Mark 8:34

32 Jude 3

33 1 Thessalonians 2:3

34 Matthew 24:1-14, 36-42

35 2 Thessalonians 2:7

36 Matthew 24:1

37 1 Peter 5:8, 1 Peter 4:12, and 1 Peter 1:7

38 1 Peter 5:8

39 2 Timothy 3:12

40 2 Thessalonians 2:17

41 Luke 6:48

42 Matthew 22:37

43 1 Corinthians 9:24

44 John 15:1-4

45 Matthew 22:39

46 1 Corinthians 12:18

47 1 Corinthians 12:21

48 Acts 2:42

49 1 Corinthians 12:7

50 Acts 2:44 and 4:32

51 1 Thessalonians 5:11-12

52 Philippians 2:2

53 Sweet, Leonard, *I Am a Follower: The Way, Truth and Life of Following Jesus,* (Nashville, Tennessee, Thomas Nelson, 2012), 54.

54 Romans 12:4-5

55 Ephesians 3:6

56 Romans 1:1-17

57 Acts 2:42

58 2 Peter 1:1-11

59 Romans 12:9-14

60 James 1:22

61 John 15:8

62 1 Corinthians 9:24

63 Hebrews 12:1

64 http://www.youtube.com/watch?v=X5dgJwEvhrA&feature=fvwrel; other version: http://www.youtube.com/watch?v=1YhP5zSicdk

65 Philippians 3:14

66 1 Corinthians 9:24

67 Galatians 5:7

68 Isaiah 6:8

Appendix Four

1 1 Samuel 31:8

2 1 Kings 18:19

3 Exodus 19

4 Joshua 8:30

5 Deuteronomy 34:1-4

6 Mark 15:22

7 Revelation 2:4-5

8 John 5:8-9

9 Joshua 24:1-28

10 John 21:1-23

11 Acts 9

12 Luke 24:49-53 and Acts 1:3-11

13 James 2:20

14 Galatians 5:6 KJV

Acknowledgements

I have to start by thanking my dear wife, Patti. From listening to my story about God calling me to write this book, to advice for the title, reading drafts, and being patient with my unforgiving schedule, she was important to the completion of this book. Thank you so much!

From the beginning, John Kenney encouraged me with this project. He gave me confidence to write in my voice and provided pointers along the way. He is an awesome pastor, visionary, and friend. Thank you, brother.

Dear pastors read through early drafts, made suggestions, and gave encouragement. Many thanks to Danny Barton, Coy Hinton, and Grady Wigley. Grady, you are a precious pastor, mentor, saint, and friend.

Many thanks to the generosity of Joey Barrs for his talent in providing some illustrations.

Great appreciation is due for the encouragement from my children in the SGJ crew: Brian and Samantha Sharp, Carleton and Claire Gallagher, and Ryan and Emily Jimenez.

Thanks to everyone on the cover design, editing, layout, and publishing team.